manifesto
THREE CLASSIC ESSAYS ON
HOW TO CHANGE THE WORLD

manifesto

THREE CLASSIC ESSAYS ON
HOW TO CHANGE THE WORLD

ERNESTO CHE GUEVARA
KARL MARX & FRIEDRICH ENGELS
ROSA LUXEMBURG

PREFACE BY ADRIENNE RICH
INTRODUCTION BY ARMANDO HART

SEVEN STORIES PRESS
new york • oakland • london

Published by Seven Stories Press on behalf of Ocean Press, Melbourne, Australia, and the Che Guevara Studies Center, Havana. Direct all rights inquiries and permissions questions to rights@sevenstories.com.

Library of Congress Cataloging-in-Publication Data is on file.

ISBN 978-1-64421-280-6 (paperback)
ISBN 978-1-64421-281-3 (e-book)

Printed in the USA

9 8 7 6 5 4 3 2 1

contents

a d r i e n n e   r i c h

"KARL MARX, ROSA LUXEMBURG AND CHE GUEVARA"

If you are curious and open to the life around you, if you are troubled as to why, how and by whom political power is held and used, if you sense there must be good intellectual reasons for your unease, if your curiosity and openness drive you toward wishing to act with others, to "do something," you already have much in common with the writers of the three essays in this book.

The essays in *Manifesto* were written by three relatively young people — Karl Marx when he was 30, Rosa Luxemburg at 27, Che Guevara at the age of 37. Born into different historical moments and different generations, they shared an energy of hope, an engagement with history, a belief that critical thinking must inform action, and a passion for the world and its human possibilities. That society as it was materially constructed would have to undergo radical change in order for such possibilities, stifled or denied under existing conditions, to be realized, all three affirmed in their lives and work. They were educated, reflective people who sharpened their thinking powers on that endeavor.

Marx lived most of his prodigiously creative life in poverty and exile. Rosa Luxemburg and Che Guevara were targeted and assassinated for their intellectual and active leadership in socialist movements. Any one of them might have led the life of a relatively comfortable professional. Each made a different choice. Yet reading what they wrote, including the essays in this book, one feels not the grimness of a tooth-gritting, dogma-driven politics, but the verve and exuberance of mind that accompanies creative indignation. For all three, feeling intensely alive translated into the vision of an integrated society, in which each person could become both individuated and socially responsible: "an association," as a famous phrase from *The Communist Manifesto* expresses it, "in which the free development of each is the condition for the free development of all."[1] Or, as Che told a group of Cuban medical students and health workers in 1960:

> The revolution is not, as some claim, a standardizer of collective will, of collective initiative. To the contrary, it is a liberator of human beings' individual capacity.
> What the revolution does do, however, is to orient that capacity.[2]

None of them was thinking in isolation or in a historical vacuum. They had the past and its earlier thinkers to learn from and critique; they observed and participated in social movements; they worked out and argued ideas and strategies, sometimes fiercely, with comrades (Marx especially with Friedrich Engels, Luxemburg with Leo Jogiches, Clara Zetkin, Karl Kautsky and others of the German Social Democratic Party, Che Guevara with Fidel Castro, other Latin Americans and with leaders of the "nonaligned" nations). They saw themselves not as "public intellectuals" but as witnesses of and contributors to the growing consciousness of a class which produced wealth and leisure without sharing in it, a class fully capable of reason and enlightened action, though often lacking the formal education that could lead to political power.

That the working people who produced the wealth of the world could move toward political and economic emancipation, they did not simply believe but saw as a necessary evolution in human history. Revolutions were all around them, mass movements, strikes, international organizing. But it was not just the temper of their times that drew them into activity. (Many professionals and writers, especially when young, have been attracted by a moment's flaring promise of social change, only to pull back as the windchill of opposition begins to freeze the air.) Rather, they observed around them the accelerating relationship between private wealth and massive suffering, capital's devouring appetite for expansion of its markets at whatever human cost (including its wars); and in that awareness they also saw the meaning of their lives.

As a young medical student traveling through Latin America, Che Guevara noted this concretely:

> I went to see an old woman with asthma… The poor thing was in a pitiful state, breathing the acrid smell of concentrated sweat and dirty feet that filled her room, mixed with the dust from a couple of armchairs, the only luxury items in her house. On top of her asthma, she had a heart condition. It is at times like this, when a doctor is conscious of his complete powerlessness, that he longs for change: a change to prevent the injustice of a system in which only a month ago this poor woman was still earning her living as a waitress, wheezing and panting but facing life with dignity.[3]

It was Marx first of all who described how capital not only dispossesses and forces the vast majority of people "to sell themselves piecemeal," but contains, ultimately, its own undoing:

> Modern bourgeois society, with its relations of production, of exchange and of property, a society that has conjured up such gigantic means of production and of exchange, is like the sorcerer, who is no longer able to control the powers of the netherworld whom he has called up by his spells.[4]

But he first lays forth an exposition of the history of capitalism, the emergence of bourgeois or owning-class power and the effects of that power, a panorama so prescient of 21st century social conditions that it transcends its own moment of writing. As Che was to observe in 1964:

The merit of Marx is that he suddenly produces a qualitative change in the history of social thought. He interprets history, understands its dynamic, foresees the future. But in addition to foreseeing it (by which he would meet his scientific obligation), he expresses a revolutionary concept: it is not enough to interpret the world, it must be transformed.[5]

And in fact, over more than 150 years *The Communist Manifesto* has become the most influential, most translated, reprinted (and demonized) single document of modern history. It's a work of extraordinary literary power fused with historical analysis; a document of its time yet resonant, as we see here, for later generations. A document which can be, has been, critiqued and argued with — even by its author — but which will be carried into any future that is bearable to contemplate.

Marx, Luxemburg and Guevara were revolutionaries but they were not romantics. Their often poetic eloquence is grounded in their study and critical analysis of human society and political economy from the earliest communistic arrangements of prehistory to the emergence of modern capitalism and imperialist wars. They did not idealize past societies or attempt to create marginal communities of lifestyle purists, but — beginning with Marx — they scrutinized the illusions of past and contemporary reformers and rebels in the light of history, aware how easy it can be for parties and leaders to lose momentum, drift off and settle down with existing relationships of power. (It is this kind of compromise that Luxemburg addresses in *Reform or Revolution*.)

So what have we here?

The Communist Manifesto was so named because at a certain moment the emerging German League of Communists asked Marx and Engels to draft a platform. Thus, Marx is both setting forth a new theory of history and making a program *manifest*: asking, what in economic history has produced the need for Communism as a movement *and* what does Communism in 1848 actually stand for? He describes, with admiration as well as condemnation, the contradictory achievements of industrial capitalism. He notes, sometimes with scorching wit, the "spectral" interpretations of Communism floating abroad, and defines its real goal as common ownership of the means of production.

Fifty years later, in 1899, Luxemburg vigorously analyzes the reformist "opportunism" that would keep the old systemic relations of ownership and production in place under the guise of socialist reform. She dissects this opportunism in the ideas of Eduard Bernstein, an elder leader of the German Marxist Social Democratic Party with the additional cachet of being Engels' literary executor. Her confrontation is coming from a young person, a foreigner, and a woman in a party rife with "virulent male chauvinism."[6] Coming from anyone, it would have constituted a brilliant intellectual autopsy.

Luxemburg makes it clear that to be antireformist is not to be antireform:

> For Social Democracy there exists an indissoluble tie between social reform and revolution. The struggle for reforms is its *means*; the social revolution, its *goal*.[7]

With her critique of Bernstein's article as a springboard, she goes on to enunciate ideas that acquire renewed pungency and suggestiveness today:

> The fate of the socialist movement is not bound to bourgeois democracy; but the fate of democracy, on the contrary, is bound to the socialist movement. Democracy does not acquire greater chances of life in the measure that the working class renounces the struggle for its emancipation; on the contrary, democracy acquires greater chances of survival as the socialist movement becomes sufficiently strong to struggle against the reactionary consequences of world politics and the bourgeois desertion of democracy. He who would strengthen democracy must also want to strengthen and not weaken the socialist movement; and with the renunciation of the struggle for socialism goes that of both the labor movement and democracy.[8]

> Legal reform and revolution are not different methods of historical progress that can be picked out at pleasure from the counter of history,

just as one chooses hot or cold sausages. They are different *moments* in the development of class society which condition and complement each other, and at the same time exclude each other reciprocally...

In effect, every legal constitution is the *product* of a revolution. In the history of classes, revolution is the act of political creation while legislation is the political expression of the life of a society that has already come into being. Work for legal reforms does not itself contain its own driving force independent from revolution.[9]

In 1965, Che Guevara, as participant-theorist of an actual ongoing revolution, writes to an Uruguayan editor friend a letter obviously intended to *make manifest* the experience of the emerging Cuban society. By then, Che, an Argentine, had traveled on his continent, studied Marxism in Guatemala, fought along with Fidel Castro and the July 26 Movement,[10] served in the new Cuban revolutionary government, and was beginning to work for the extension of socialism in Latin America and among the "nonaligned" nations of Africa and Asia. He is writing of the labor pains of a transitional revolutionary society. How is it to be born? There is the idea, socialism, and there is also "the human being" — incomplete, coming alive in new conditions where labor becomes shared social responsibility, but also initially dwelling as it were between two vastly different worlds: "The new society in formation has to compete fiercely with the past."[11] Commodity relationships are still imprinted on the mind. This phase of revolutionary process is new and unstable and anxiety may seek relief in autocratic rigidity. The leadership in such a transition has need for a vigilant, well-calibrated self-criticism. Rosa Luxemburg had written: "Revolutions are not 'made' and great movements of the people are not produced according to technical recipes that repose in the pockets of the party leaders."[12] Che envisioned that "[s]ociety as a whole must be converted into a gigantic school"[13]; those who hope to educate must be in constant and responsive touch with those who are learning: teachers must also be learners.

In this connection it's necessary to think about art and culture. Marx writes of how the bourgeoisie cannot exist without constantly revolutionizing the instruments of production, and thereby the relations of production, and with them the whole relations of society... [U]ninterrupted disturbance of all social conditions, everlasting uncertainty and agitation distinguish the bourgeois epoch from all earlier ones. All fixed, fast-frozen relations, with their train of ancient and venerable prejudices and opinions, are swept away, all new-formed ones become antiquated before they can ossify. All that is solid melts into air...[14]

And, in a system of commodity relationships, "the physician, the lawyer, the priest, the poet, the man of science" become "paid wage laborers" who must "sell themselves piecemeal" and "are consequently exposed to all the vicissitudes of exploitation, all the fluctuations of the market." For the artist, this can also mean censorship by the market.

Che elaborates this theme:

The superstructure [of capitalism] imposes a kind of art in which the artist must be educated. Rebels are subdued by the machine, and only exceptional talents [I read this phrase as in ironic quotes] may create their own work. The rest become shamefaced hirelings or are crushed... Meaningless anguish or vulgar amusement thus become convenient safety valves for human anxiety. The idea of using art as a weapon of protest is combated.[15]

But he also points to the blinders of earlier socialist revolutions-in-process, where "an exaggerated dogmatism" has tried to address the question of culture, demanding "the formally exact representation of nature" in art, followed by "a mechanical representation of the social reality they wanted to show: the ideal society, almost without conflicts or contradictions, that they sought to create."[16]

Che struggles here with the dialectic of art as simultaneously embodiment and shaper of consciousness, rooted in past forms and materials even as it gestures toward a still unachieved reality. What is to be the freedom of the artist in the new Cuba? It can be difficult, living under present conditions, to conceive of how a freedom expanded to all, to each and every person, might expand, not limit, the freedom of the imaginative artist, and the very possibilities of art. Difficult for those who are already artists — even as, outraged, we are forced to market ourselves piecemeal and struggle for what Marx called "disposable time"[17] — to see the "invisible cage" within which we work. Difficult, too, perhaps, for the navigators of a new society to apprehend the peculiar, but not exceptional, labor of the artist.

In the words of the Italian Communist Antonio Gramsci:

> ...to be precise, one should speak of a struggle for a "new culture" and not for a "new art" (in the immediate sense)... [P]erhaps it cannot even be said that the struggle is for a new artistic content apart from form because content cannot be considered abstractly, in separation from form. To fight for a new art would mean to fight to create new individual artists, which is absurd since artists cannot be created artificially. One must speak of a struggle for a new culture, that is, for a new moral life that cannot but be intimately connected to a new intuition of life, until it becomes a new way of feeling and seeing reality and, therefore, a world intimately engrained in "possible artists" and "possible works of art."[18]

The serious revolutionary, like the serious artist, can't afford to lead a self-indulgent or self-deceiving life. Patience, realism and critical imagination are required of both kinds of creativity. Yet all the writers in this book speak emotionally of the human condition and of human realization, not as "losing oneself" within a mass collectivity but as release from the frozen senses, the dumbed-down alienation of mass society: Marx of "the complete *emancipation* of all the human qualities and senses [from the mere sense of *having*]... The eye has become a *human* eye when its object has become a *human,* social object"[19]; Rosa Luxemburg of "social happiness," of the mass strike as "creativity," of "freedom" as no "special privilege" and of the "love of every beautiful day." And Che of the revolutionary as "moved by great feelings of love" though this may "seem ridiculous" in bourgeois politics; of the need for a "new human being" created through responsible participation in a society belonging to all.

As Aijaz Ahmad has written, "The first resource of hope is memory itself."[20] Marxism is founded on the historical memory of how existing, apparently immutable, human relationships came to be as they are. In the essays that follow we hear voices from three different generations of people who believed, as recent enormous antiwar and anti-imperialist gatherings on every continent have been asserting, that "another world is possible." If for some today this still only means trying to regulate and refurbish the runaway engine of capitalism, for an ever-growing number of others it means changing the direction of the journey, toward an utterly different, still-forming reality. Here are urgent conversations from the past that are still being carried on, among new voices, throughout the world.

Adrienne Rich
March 2004

---

1. see Karl Marx and Friedrich Engels, *The Communist Manifesto*, in this edition, p53.

2. Ernesto Che Guevara, "Speech to Medical Students and Health Workers," *Che Guevara Reader* (New York: Seven Stories Press, 2022), p115.

3. Ernesto Che Guevara, *The Motorcycle Diaries* (New York: Seven Stories Press, 2021), p70.

4. see *The Communist Manifesto*, in this edition, p35.

5. "Notes for the Study of the Ideology of the Cuban Revolution," *Che Guevara Reader*, p123.

6. Raya Dunayevskaya, *Rosa Luxemburg, Women's Liberation and Marx's Philosophy of Revolution*, 2nd ed. (Champaign: University of Illinois Press, 1991), p27.

7. see *Reform or Revolution*, in this edition, p71.

8. see *Reform or Revolution*, in this edition, p126.

9. see *Reform or Revolution*, in this edition, p128.

10. The revolutionary movement led by Fidel Castro that overthrew the regime of Fulgencio Batista in Cuba (1959). Its name commemorated Fidel's July 26, 1953, attack on the Moncada army barracks.

11. see *Socialism and Man in Cuba*, in this edition, p154.

12. Peter Hudis and Kevin B. Anderson, eds., *The Rosa Luxemburg Reader* (New York: Monthly Review Press, 2004), p328.

13. see *Socialism and Man in Cuba*, in this edition, p155.

14. see *The Communist Manifesto*, in this edition, p33.

15. see *Socialism and Man in Cuba*, in this edition, p161.

16. see *Socialism and Man in Cuba*, in this edition, p162.

17. Karl Marx, *Grundrisse: Foundations of the Critique of Political Economy*, tr. Martin Nicolaus (New York: Penguin USA, 1983), p708.

18. Antonio Gramsci, *Selections from Cultural Writings*, David Forgacs and Geoffrey Nowell-Smith, eds., tr. William Boelhower (Cambridge MA: Harvard University Press, 1985), p98.

19. "Private Property and Communism," *The Portable Karl Marx*, Eugene Kamenka, ed. (New York: Penguin USA, 1983), p151.

20. "Resources of Hope: A Reflection on Our Times," in *Frontline* (India) Vol. 18 #10, May 15–25, 2001.

INTRODUCTION

armando hart

José Martí spoke of the invisible threads linking human beings across history. The publication of these three texts together: *The Communist Manifesto* by Marx and Engels, *Reform or Revolution* by Rosa Luxemburg and *Socialism and Man in Cuba* by Ernesto Che Guevara — all written in vastly different eras: 1848, 1899 and 1965 — will direct the reader to these invisible threads that bring together socialist ideas of the 19th and 20th centuries.

If we were capable of publishing and studying the fundamental texts on the nature of socialism, by a range of authors, we would discover increasingly profound answers to the real causes of the failure of the left in the 20th century. This has become a need that can no longer be postponed, because in the 20th century, following Lenin's death, the essential principles of Marx and Lenin have been adulterated, whittled away. Humanity cannot advance toward a new type of thinking in the 21st century if the essence of the works of these geniuses is not clarified.

The common essence of these three texts, brought together in this book, is the aspiration of human redemption in "the kingdom of this world," and achieving this redemption with the aid of science, by raising consciousness and by mobilizing the poor and exploited in the world. These texts represent an indictment of human alienation born out of the exploitation of human by human. Likewise, they have in common the idea that the capitalist system leads, as a result of its own development, to the need to find ways of socializing wealth.

A detailed analysis of these texts allows us to understand in greater depth that, after Lenin's death, the political importance of culture was not integrated into socialist practice. It was not taken into account by Engels when... he pointed out:

> ...Civilization has achieved things of which gentile society was not even remotely capable. But it achieved them by setting in motion the lowest instincts and passions in man and developing them at the expense of all his other abilities. From its first day to this, sheer greed was the driving spirit of civilization; wealth and again wealth and once more wealth, wealth, not of society, but of the single miserable individual — here was its one and final aim. If at the same time the progressive development of science and a repeated flowering of supreme art dropped into its lap, it was only because without them modern wealth could not have completely realized its achievements.[1]

Socialism therefore demands the promotion of the best in human nature, and to this end it is essential to find and utilize the ideas of key cultural figures. It is crucial to select the ideas and thoughts of all the greatest cultural figures from the era of the mythical Prometheus to contemporary times. This can be done using the selective methods of Cuban cultural traditions — methods chosen precisely to find the paths to justice.

We continue to insist that the thoughts of a wise person are not enough on their own to find the path to socialism. Moreover, the infinite wisdom of great socialist thinkers is not enough to open the gateway to these redemptory ideas that, say what you might, are the most profound and sophisticated to emerge from Europe and have acquired the greatest significance over the last two centuries. As we have mentioned to the publishers, we see this book only as a first endeavor toward something more ambitious. We must continue to seek the invisible threads in order to articulate contemporary fragmented culture, or the process of the dissolution of what is known as western civilization.

It is essential to clear away the mysteries of current neoliberal fragmentation — of the anarchy and chaos prevailing in the world — an argument dramatically expressed by Fidel Castro on the 45th anniversary of the Cuban Revolution: "Either the course of events must change or our species will not be able to survive."[2]

As Cubans we can grasp the essence of universal culture expressed in these texts because we have been able to perceive what has transcended from them. This is fundamental for humanity today. That we are able to interpret it within a contemporary context, on the basis of the teachings and traditions of major figures from our history, of whom José Martí is the most outstanding, is due to our experience of the revolution of January 1, 1959. In other words, we have 45 years of practice in confrontation and struggle against the most powerful empire in the world.

Moving in chronological order, I want to set out what I consider to be the key aspects of the documents we are presenting to the reader.

The first of these is, naturally, *The Communist Manifesto*, written, as is well known, by Marx and Engels in 1848. It begins with the famous words, "A spectre is haunting Europe...," to which I might add: this spectre has remained at the center of history for 150 years. We could also state that since 1848 no political event has been without direct or indirect relation to the fire of ideas and feelings which this text evoked. In one way or another, the text has been present in the historical subconscious of western civilization, either to support or to undermine it. Of even greater importance is that it has been present, over the past 150 years, in the interweaving of redemptory ideas and aspirations that have been at the heart of western civilization. What we have to ask ourselves is whether humanity is capable of forgetting, of pushing to the side, the hopes and emancipatory aspirations that are framed by the communist ideal.

The *Manifesto* was written to describe and denounce the capitalist social regime in mid-19th century Europe. No political document written since has achieved this with such depth and clarity, or so faithfully expressed the revolutionary needs of its historical period. It described with scientific depth and literary quality the essence of social and economic history since remote antiquity up to its time; and no other document of its kind has improved on its analysis. Without the lessons it provides, the subsequent development of history in the second half of the 19th century and the whole of the 20th century could not be understood.

During the trial of those involved in the July 26, 1953, attack on the Moncada garrison, the state prosecutor accused Fidel Castro of being criminal for the fact of keeping books by Lenin in the apartment of Haydée and Abel Santamaría.[3] Fidel responded: "Those interested in politics who have not read and studied Lenin are ignorant." Moved by Fidel's words, I resolved to embark upon an in-depth study of Marx, Engels and Lenin. After more than 50 years, I can say that those interested in politics who have not read *The Communist Manifesto* of 1848 are also ignorant. Those who, like Fidel, study it and learn from its teachings, and at the same time embrace the cause of the poor, will find the path to revolution.

Reading *The Communist Manifesto*, with the benefit of experience acquired through events of the past century and a half, we can see that the authors not only described profoundly and concisely the historical period in which the text was written, they also provided invaluable teachings for the world in which we live today.

The reader, by viewing humanity's development since then through the key lines in the *Manifesto*, will see that capitalism has continued to march toward taking control of the surplus value created by human labor, which it still extracts from workers. The theft has continued, it is more widespread and has been carried out in a more dramatic fashion. To the extent that we are capable of making an abstraction without prejudice, it enables us to interpret the concrete facts we have within sight and confirm that capitalist society is jeopardizing the relations of production that the system itself has created.

It is clear that modern bourgeois society, which has emerged from the ruins of feudal society, has continued to march forward amid the contradictions and antagonisms that it generated and never abolished. Instead, all it has done is to continue substituting the old conditions of oppression; it is evident that socioeconomic antagonisms and the exploitation of human labor have become increasingly threatening to humanity's future on earth. It may be demonstrated that wherever bourgeois power has existed, it has continued to transform the relations of production into an alienating factor that makes individual freedom a simple commercial asset. It has substituted the numerous structured freedoms with inhuman and soulless market freedoms. Put simply, instead of exploitation clouded by political or religious illusions, bourgeois power has continued to establish open, direct and brutal exploitation.

Doctors, legal experts, priests, poets and scientists have, over the past 150 years, become its paid servants. It has continued to wipe away the emotions and feelings that in the past have characterized social relationships, reducing them to simple financial relations. Likewise, it will be understood that the bourgeoisie cannot exist unless it is to transform unceasingly the instruments and relations of production and, consequently, social relations in general. It has continued to eliminate all that is simple and timeless, all that is sacred it has made profane, and human beings have been compelled to analyze the nature of their real social relations.

Study *The Communist Manifesto* as though it were a valuable historical document giving the background necessary to gain insights into and better confront the realities of the present and the future. Compare it with what has happened in the past 150 years and the reader will see that essential truths in the text have been confirmed and exemplified in increasingly dramatic ways by life itself.

Let us see: If this study has been carried out in an unbiased fashion, it will reveal that the course of social and political events confirms that to the present day, the history of society continues to be a struggle between oppressor and oppressed, engaged in *eternal confrontation,* sometimes veiled, but otherwise direct and open. There is a crucial warning here for all human beings inhabiting the earth and particularly for those involved in making decisions: these struggles have always ended with the victory of one or other of the belligerent classes, with the revolutionary transformation of the entire society or with the collapse of the classes involved in the confrontation. This idea torments us and is the key question in the world of the 21st century.

In short, *The Communist Manifesto* invites us to reflect on the truths it sets out. With this in mind, those who have read this famous document should read it once again. If you have not yet done so, read it for the first time. You will always find it a useful guide to understanding the historic drama of exploited peoples and as a lesson in the struggle for human and social emancipation.

We can say today, paraphrasing Engels, that *The Communist Manifesto* is one of the greatest documents ever written in support of the poor of the earth in favor of their struggle for liberation. We could begin to discuss his ideas using the profoundly ethical thinking of José Martí, when he said, in relation to Karl Marx: "He deserves to be honored for declaring himself on the side of the weak."[4]

Let's move on to comment on Rosa Luxemburg's text. From an intellectual point of view and particularly within the terrain of social sciences, history and philosophy, she is one of the most outstanding women in the world and among the elevated intellectuals of the human race. With her assassination on January 15, 1919, the right wing demonstrated its powerful class instinct and proved that it was more aware of the caliber and significance of unswerving revolutionaries than many who proclaimed themselves as such.

Rosa fought equally against reformism as she did against dogmatism, meaning that she made enemies among dogmatists and reformists. As it was both sides that imposed themselves on the evolution of socialist ideas in the 20th century, the illustrious adopted daughter of the Germany of Marx and Engels was smothered under the tapestry of false interpretations of these founding fathers' work.

Much was lost to the world revolutionary movement with the assassination of Rosa Luxemburg and the marginalization of her luminous ideas. Until now we have been arguing the importance of the subjective factor in history, in a progressive sense. The dramatic reality of contemporary times has shown that this same factor also impacts negatively as a painful historical lesson. In relation to Rosa Luxemburg's ideas, we have a sound judgment to make in this respect.

In this text Rosa criticizes reformist statements from a dialectical perspective and in terms that are logically rigorous. She points out how positions originating from these statements exacerbated contradictions between the rich and the poor and led to the need for a social revolution. The 100 years that have passed since she wrote this text demonstrate that reformism, far from succeeding, helped to universalize anarchy, wars, brutal conflicts, and even to expand terrorism throughout the globe, creating the particularly grave situation we currently face in the world.

The basic argument put forward by reformists in the times of Marx, Engels and Lenin and, consequently, in Rosa Luxemburg's era, stated that capitalism could cushion and even overcome class differences with measures such as the following:

- Improvements in the situation of the working class

- Extension and broadening of credit

- Development of the key means of transport

- Concentration of the trusts that accentuated the tendency toward the socialization of the means of production

For reformists, these processes would blunt the class contradictions that would lead to social upheaval and, therefore, to a revolution against capitalism. The position set out by Rosa Luxemburg was that these processes could slow down or delay and, as a consequence, lengthen the workers' struggle, but that in the end social chaos was inevitable.

How are the weaknesses of these reformist theses manifested? If capitalists were people without petty ambitions and were educated, or at least had common sense, the ideal situation would naturally be a process of reforms. Yet this doctrine fails because, as Martí said: "All men are sleeping dragons. It is necessary to rein in the dragon. Man is an admirable dragon: he has been given his own reins." The key then is in the triumph of common sense, intelligence and culture. We Cubans know this because of our ethical, juridical, social and political traditions of universal value.

What is certain is that the failure of reformists is due not to the possible logical value of their statements, but to the objective fact that the petty and short-term interests of the owners of wealth prevail over more elemental truths than logic. Moreover, these essential truths that, as I say, are rooted in common sense, will lead them to consistently apply reformist ideas; but the [reformist] process will not take place because evil, mediocrity and petty interests rule in the minds of the principal owners of wealth.[5] All social systems have disappeared on account of this mixture of stupidity, mediocrity and evil.

In another of her works known as the *Junius Pamphlet*, Rosa Luxemburg formulates a political slogan and historical choice that faces humanity: *socialism or barbarism*. More than 80 years after her death, history has dramatically proven her to be correct.

Today's dilemma is that, for the time being, barbarism has imposed itself. It can only be substituted, from our perspective, by a line of march that, in the final analysis, leads to socialism.

Today we live in a world that is described as *globalized*; I say globalized because of what the Spanish writer Ramón Fernández Durán called the *explosion of disorder*. A revolutionary process must take into account objective and economic factors, but it must also consider the cultural and moral questions involved. The basic error of 20th century Marxist interpretation, after Lenin, was precisely in neglecting this key element in political practice.

Finally, we will deal with the well-known text by Ernesto Che Guevara. An analysis of this allows us to explore Che's central idea: the role of subjectivity and, therefore, of culture in socialism and the education of the new human being.

Socialism and Man in Cuba encourages us, as the most recent of the documents published here, to reflect on the challenges facing socialism. In this text, an embryonic analysis of the superstructural and subjective factors in relation to the material base of socialist society is presented. Hence, it continues to be a key text which contemporary revolutionaries must study in depth.

In this text, Che broaches the crucial question of the ideological, political, moral and cultural superstructure and its relations with the economic base in the specific Cuban situation of the early years of the revolution. He highlights that socialism was only infant in terms of the development of long-term economic and political theory. All that he outlined was tentative, he stated, because it required subsequent elaboration, which did not happen. In an era when material incentives were promoted to achieve social mobilization and intensify production, Che insisted on means and methods of a moral character, without neglecting the correct use of material incentives, particularly of a social nature.

This is, precisely, the Cuban Revolution's contribution to socialist ideas and it does not contradict the ideas of Marx, Engels and Lenin.

Forty years ago, he raised the problem of direct creation, in other words, the immediate results of humanity's productive activity. Today, we must study Che's ideas and suggestions from a broader and more general perspective of culture.

Over four decades later, the matter of subjectivity and, therefore, of ethics, is revealed to us in a more complete and defined way. Today it is inseparable from Fidel Castro's proposal to attain a comprehensive level of culture in society. The culture of emancipation and accordingly, Che's ideas on subjectivity, are of immediate interest in our process of revolutionary analysis of the influence of culture in socioeconomic development. This is the only way to find the path that leads to new philosophical thinking and to political action in tune with the contemporary situation.

Determining the influence of culture in development is fundamental to elaborate the ideas needed in the 21st century, especially in the Americas. To test the importance of culture in the economy is an unavoidable commitment we have with Ernesto Che Guevara. This would demand a more detailed analysis, but for now we are going to refer to the matter that Che raised, that of subjectivity. To carry out this analysis, one has to begin with the question of culture and its influence on the history of humanity. This matter has remained pending in the history of socialist ideas during the 20th century.

Let me discuss, by way of a conclusion, some reflections on the role of culture. I will do this by beginning with the history of civilizations in order to reach later more concrete conclusions. A starting point would be the opinion that in the history of civilizations, the theft and misrepresentation of culture has been the principal maneuver of the exploiters in order to impose their selfish interests on others. If this is not understood then the essence of the problem is not understood.

The introduction of the social question as the essential theme in culture is relatively recent in the history of our civilization. It was precisely Marx and Engels who, with great coherence and rigor, placed this question at the forefront of western thinking.

Until then, philosophy had existed in order to interpret the world, but from Marx and Engels the argument emerged for the need to change it. There is no philosophical and practical conclusion of greater importance for humanity in its millennial history. On studying the documents we present here, the reader will therefore understand that we have published them with the essential aim of encouraging a search for ideas that will be useful in finding the paths to revolutionary transformation.

In order to achieve this, we must begin with the authors' own logic; otherwise we will not be able to discover what their contribution was and where the essential limits to all human achievements are. This is about appreciating an undeniable cultural value. We come across major difficulties. Both the practical application of Marx and Engels' thinking over recent decades, and enemy propaganda about their ideas — the vision of a closed doctrine with roots in rigid philosophical determinism — was imposed on the consciousness of millions of people. Those who, from the conservative or reactionary ranks, refuted Marx and Engels' thinking, accusing them of just these same tendencies, or those who also, consciously or unconsciously, attempted to do so from beneath revolutionary banners, were guilty of the same mistake. The only difference is that the former have been more consistent in their interests than the latter.

The philosophical essence of the renowned writers of these texts is, precisely, the exact opposite of dogmatic rigidity. It is really paradoxical that philosophical thinking will only free itself from the vicious circle it is trapped in when Marx and Engels are studied and interpreted in a manner radically different from that prevalent in the 20th century, after Lenin's death. In other words, when their thinking is approached as "a research method" and as a "guide to action" that does not aspire to reveal "eternal truths" but to orienting and encouraging the social liberation of humanity on the basis of the interests of the poor and exploited of the world. Those who followed this route in 20th century history generated real social revolutions, as in the case of Lenin, Ho Chi Minh and Fidel Castro. Those who interpreted Marx and Engels' works as irrefutable dogma did not attain these heights; on the contrary, they made them into lifeless texts remote from reality.

An important lesson that can be learnt from this is that the value of a culture may be gauged by its power of assimilation and capacity to excel in the face of new realities. The ideas of intellectuals in all the sciences, including those of a socio-historical nature, are of no value on their own. Their value lies in their potential to discover, on the basis of new findings, new truths. The highest levels of thinking and significant new ideas are cornerstones of the building humanity is constructing in the history of culture, whose foundations are constantly moving and experiencing change. They are not the building, but the key to opening its doors and orienting us toward its interior. Their importance lies in resisting the test of time and retaining a value beyond the immediate, because they manage to synthesize the elements necessary to satisfy needs in social and historical evolution. They are changing the way in which they appear. Those who have contributed to science and culture have done so because they have been able to weave what is new into the tapestry of history.

All cultures that engage in an exploration of the ideal of justice among human beings, if this is done so in depth and with rigor, will penetrate human consciousness and find one of the keys to universal history.

To promote the redemptory ideas contained within these texts it is necessary to study what has turned out to be different from the suppositions on which the ideas of Marxism, outlined in these pages, were founded. Their evaluations were essentially grounded in European reality. Nothing other than this could have been demanded from them. The best of European revolutionary thinking in the 19th century did not arise from a Eurocentric vision.

The expansion of the United States and its ascent to become a powerful capitalist country following the War of Secession [Civil War] on the one hand, in addition to the mass migration from the Old World to North America in the final decades of the 19th century and the beginning of the 20th century on the other, were historic milestones allowing us to grasp the scope and form that these phenomena would subsequently assume.

If we study a letter from Marx to [Abraham] Lincoln, his hope that the outbreak of war between the North and South would become a step toward a future proletarian revolution in that country is apparent. This did not happen. The European pressure cooker did not explode, among other reasons because the potential labor force in Europe found new markets in North American territories at the end of the 19th century and during the course of the 20th century.

Friedrich Engels said that Hegel's most important discoveries were due to the degree of his knowledge of his era and that his limitations were also appropriate to his times. It has to be pointed out that the vast knowledge in 19th century Europe, which we admire as one of the highest pinnacles of western culture, was ignorant of and did not ever value the United States, much less the growing revolutionary potential of Latin America.

The following thoughts by Engels are very illustrative of this: "The social and economic phases that these countries [referring to the Third World] will also have to go through before attaining social organization cannot be, I believe, anything other than the object of quite idle speculations. One thing is certain, the victorious proletariat cannot impose happiness on a foreign people without compromising its own victory." This lesson has been proven dramatically in the reality of the very heart of the old continent.

Marx and Engels did not take into account the imperialist phases studied by Lenin, nor were they sufficiently well acquainted with the socioeconomic realities facing Third World countries. Neither was the founder of the October Revolution able to study our continent, although his analysis of imperialism focused on the main problem of the 20th century, and was based on information he had acquired on the liberation process that was developing during that period among the people of Asia.

The rescue of the best traditions within universal culture is an undeniable means of defending the interests of the poor. It is should be compulsory to carry out concrete economic studies that help us demonstrate reliably that culture has been the most dynamic factor in the economic history of the world, and particularly the world within which we are living.

In order to explore the question in some depth I suggest following the thread linking these documents historically on the basis of José Martí's most central ideas. When we read Martí, we begin to notice a more detailed analysis of the reasons why socialism failed. He was fulfilling the role of prophet when he warned of the following:

> There is something I must praise highly, and it is the affection you show in your dealings with people; and your masculine respect for Cubans, whoever they might be, who are out there sincerely seeking a world that is a little better and an essential balance in the administration of this world's affairs. Such an aspiration must be judged as noble, regardless of whatever extremes human passion might take it to. The socialist project, like many others, involves two dangers: readings that are confused and incomplete, distancing the project from reality; and the concealed pride and anger of the ambitious, who make pretences in order to get ahead in the world, to have shoulders to hoist themselves on, frenetic defenders of the helpless. Some go like pests, the queen's hangers on, as was Marat when with green ink he dedicated his book to her, bloody flattery, Marat's egg of justice. Others go like lunatics or chamberlains, like those Chateaubriand spoke of in his *Memoirs*. But the risk is not as great among our people as it is in those societies which are more wrathful, where there is less natural light. Our job is to explain simply and in detail, as you know how to: it is not to compromise sublime justice by using flawed methods or making excessive demands. And always with justice, you and I, because mistakes that are made do not authorize those with good souls to desert in its defense. Very well then, there it is, May 1. I anxiously await your account.[6]

Martí represents a humanist vein from within a radical tradition. His originality lies in the fact that he was radical and at the same time determined to gather the largest number of people possible in support of the cause he had in mind.

Very often human beings have been radical and have not made a sufficient mental effort to unite all those who could potentially support them. On other occasions they have endeavored to unite large numbers of people without being radical. Martí was radical and at the same time promoted a policy aimed at overcoming the Machiavellian principle of *divide and conquer,* replacing it with the postulate *unite to win.*

At this point we touch on an essential matter within the Cuban intellectual tradition: the role of culture and ethics in society. On the philosophical plane, Martí pointed out ideas that could lead to a crucible of principles of major political significance, practice and teaching: *the balance of the world / the still uncertain balance in the world,*[7] the *utility of virtue*[8] and the culture of making politics.

Faced with the demagogy and evil intent of those who govern the United States — those who have spoken of an "axis of evil" that includes Cuba — we could reply that it is necessary to strive toward an axis of good that consists of culture, ethics, law and political solidarity. With that framework and in the context of the Cuban Revolution, we have read and assimilated these documents that have transcended their historical times to become a vast source of wisdom, without which it would be impossible to understand our historical times and the future of the 21st century.

Armando Hart
September 2004

---

1. Friedrich Engels, "Chapter IX: Barbarism and Civilization," *The Origin of the Family, Private Property and the State,* at: http://www.marxists.org/archive/marx/works/1884/origin-family/ch09.htm.

2. Fidel Castro, *Granma* (Cuba), January 5, 2004.

3. Haydée and Abel Santamaría both participated, along with Fidel Castro, in the July 26, 1953, assault on Fulgencio Batista's Moncada army garrison. Abel Santamaría was brutally tortured and killed in the days after the attack. Haydée Santamaría was imprisoned along with other survivors.

4. José Martí, "The Memorial Meeting in Honor of Karl Marx," *José Martí Reader: Writings on the Americas* (New York: Seven Stories Press, 2024), p43.

5. José Martí, "Comentario al libro de Rafael de Castro Palomino," *Obras Completas* (Havana: Ciencias Sociales, 1993), p110.

6. José Martí, "Carta a Fermín Valdés Domínguez," *Obras Completas*, p168.

7. José Martí, "Manifesto of Montecristi," *José Martí Reader: Writings on the Americas*, p185.

8. José Martí, "Ismaelillo," *Obras Completas*.

the communist manifesto

KARL MARX & FRIEDRICH ENGELS

In 1847 Karl Marx and Friedrich Engels were asked by the newly formed League of Communists to write a manifesto outlining its aims and policies. After a series of drafts, the *Manifesto of the Communist Party* (known since 1872 as *The Communist Manifesto*) was published in February 1848. This first edition was published in German and printed in London. Prior to 1871, the year of the Paris Commune, there were only two limited editions available in Swedish and English. However, the publication of a new German edition sparked a wave of massive circulation of *The Communist Manifesto* over the decades that followed. Several prefaces were subsequently written by Marx and Engels.

A SPECTRE IS HAUNTING EUROPE — the spectre of Communism. All the powers of old Europe have entered into a holy alliance to exorcise this spectre: Pope and Czar, Metternich and Guizot, French Radicals and German police spies.

Where is the party in opposition that has not been decried as communistic by its opponents in power? Where is the opposition that has not hurled back the branding reproach of Communism, against the more advanced opposition parties, as well as against its reactionary adversaries?

Two things result from this fact:

1. Communism is already acknowledged by all European powers to be itself a power.

2. It is high time that Communists should openly, in the face of the whole world, publish their views, their aims, their tendencies, and meet this nursery tale of the Spectre of Communism with a manifesto of the party itself.

To this end, Communists of various nationalities have assembled in London and sketched the following manifesto, to be published in the English, French, German, Italian, Flemish and Danish languages.

I. BOURGEOIS AND PROLETARIANS[1]

The history of all hitherto existing society[2] is the history of class struggles.

Freeman and slave, patrician and plebeian, lord and serf, guild-master[3] and journeyman, in a word, oppressor and oppressed, stood in constant opposition to one another, carried on an uninterrupted, now hidden, now open fight, a fight that each time ended, either in a revolutionary reconstitution of society at large, or in the common ruin of the contending classes.

In the earlier epochs of history, we find almost everywhere a complicated arrangement of society into various orders, a manifold gradation of social rank. In ancient Rome we have patricians, knights, plebeians, slaves; in the Middle Ages, feudal lords, vassals, guild-masters, journeymen, apprentices, serfs; in almost all of these classes, again, subordinate gradations.

The modern bourgeois society that has sprouted from the ruins of feudal society has not done away with class antagonisms. It has but established new classes, new conditions of oppression, new forms of struggle in place of the old ones.

Our epoch, the epoch of the bourgeoisie, possesses, however, this distinctive feature: it has simplified class antagonisms. Society as a whole is more and more splitting up into two great hostile camps, into two great classes directly facing each other: bourgeoisie and pro-letariat.

From the serfs of the Middle Ages sprang the chartered burghers of the earliest towns. From these burgesses the first elements of the bourgeoisie were developed.

The discovery of America, the rounding of the Cape, opened up fresh ground for the rising bourgeoisie. The East Indian and Chinese markets, the colonization of America, trade with the colonies, the in-crease in the means of exchange and in commodities generally, gave to commerce, to navigation, to industry, an impulse never before known, and thereby, to the revolutionary element in the tottering feudal society, a rapid development.

The feudal system of industry, in which industrial production was monopolized by closed guilds, now no longer sufficed for the growing wants of the new markets. The manufacturing system took its place. The guild-masters were pushed aside by the manufacturing middle class; division of labor between the different corporate guilds vanished in the face of division of labor in each single workshop.

Meantime, the markets kept ever growing, the demand ever rising. Even manufacture no longer sufficed. Thereupon, steam and machinery revolutionized industrial production. The place of manufacture was taken by the giant, modern industry; the place of the industrial middle class by industrial millionaires, the leaders of the whole industrial armies, the modern bourgeois.

Modern industry has established the world market, for which the discovery of America paved the way. This market has given an immense development to commerce, to navigation, to communication by land. This development has, in turn, reacted on the extension of industry; and in proportion as industry, commerce, navigation, railways extended, in the same proportion the bourgeoisie developed, increased its capital, and pushed into the background every class handed down from the Middle Ages.

We see, therefore, how the modern bourgeoisie is itself the product of a long course of development, of a series of revolutions in the modes of production and of exchange.

Each step in the development of the bourgeoisie was accompanied by a corresponding political advance in that class. An oppressed class under the sway of the feudal nobility, an armed and self-governing association in the medieval commune[4]; here independent urban republic (as in Italy and Germany), there taxable "third estate" of the monarchy (as in France); afterward, in the period of manufacture proper, serving either the semifeudal or the absolute monarchy as a counterpoise against the nobility, and, in fact, cornerstone of the great monarchies

in general — the bourgeoisie has at last, since the establishment of
modern industry and of the world market, conquered for itself, in the
modern representative state, exclusive political sway. The executive of
the modern state is but a committee for managing the common affairs
of the whole bourgeoisie.

The bourgeoisie, historically, has played a most revolutionary
part.

The bourgeoisie, wherever it has got the upper hand, has put an end
to all feudal, patriarchal, idyllic relations. It has pitilessly torn asunder
the motley feudal ties that bound man to his "natural superiors," and
has left remaining no other nexus between man and man than naked
self-interest, than callous "cash payment." It has drowned the most
heavenly ecstasies of religious fervor, of chivalrous enthusiasm, of
philistine sentimentalism, in the icy water of egotistical calculation. It
has resolved personal worth into exchange value, and in place of the
numberless indefeasible chartered freedoms, has set up that single,
unconscionable freedom — free trade. In one word, for exploitation,
veiled by religious and political illusions, it has substituted naked,
shameless, direct, brutal exploitation.

The bourgeoisie has stripped of its halo every occupation hitherto
honored and looked up to with reverent awe. It has converted the
physician, the lawyer, the priest, the poet, the man of science, into its
paid wage laborers.

The bourgeoisie has torn away from the family its sentimental veil,
and has reduced the family relation to a mere money relation.

The bourgeoisie has disclosed how it came to pass that the brutal
display of vigor in the Middle Ages, which reactionaries so much
admire, found its fitting complement in the most slothful indolence. It
has been the first to show what man's activity can bring about. It has
accomplished wonders far surpassing Egyptian pyramids, Roman aq-
ueducts, and Gothic cathedrals; it has conducted expeditions that put
in the shade all former exoduses of nations and crusades.

The bourgeoisie cannot exist without constantly revolutionizing the instruments of production, and thereby the relations of production, and with them the whole relations of society. Conservation of the old modes of production in unaltered form, was, on the contrary, the first condition of existence for all earlier industrial classes. Constant revolutionizing of production, uninterrupted disturbance of all social conditions, everlasting uncertainty and agitation distinguish the bourgeois epoch from all earlier ones. All fixed, fast-frozen relations, with their train of ancient and venerable prejudices and opinions, are swept away, all new-formed ones become antiquated before they can ossify. All that is solid melts into air, all that is holy is profaned, and man is at last compelled to face with sober senses his real condition of life and his relations with his kind.

The need of a constantly expanding market for its products chases the bourgeoisie over the entire surface of the globe. It must nestle everywhere, settle everywhere, establish connections everywhere.

The bourgeoisie has, through its exploitation of the world market, given a cosmopolitan character to production and consumption in every country. To the great chagrin of reactionaries, it has drawn from under the feet of industry the national ground on which it stood. All old-established national industries have been destroyed or are daily being destroyed. They are dislodged by new industries, whose introduction becomes a life and death question for all civilized nations, by industries that no longer work up indigenous raw material, but raw material drawn from the remotest zones; industries whose products are consumed, not only at home, but in every quarter of the globe. In place of the old wants, satisfied by the production of the country, we find new wants, requiring for their satisfaction the products of distant lands and climes. In place of the old local and national seclusion and self-sufficiency, we have intercourse in every direction, universal interdependence of nations. And as in material, so also in intellectual production. The intellectual creations of individual nations become common property. National one-sidedness and narrow-mindedness become more and more impossible, and from the numerous national and local literatures, there arises a world literature.

The bourgeoisie, by the rapid improvement of all instruments of production, by the immensely facilitated means of communication, draws all, even the most barbarian, nations into civilization. The cheap prices of its commodities are the heavy artillery with which it batters down all Chinese walls, with which it forces the barbarians' intensely obstinate hatred of foreigners to capitulate. It compels all nations, on pain of extinction, to adopt the bourgeois mode of production; it compels them to introduce what it calls civilization into their midst, i.e., to become bourgeois themselves. In one word, it creates a world after its own image.

The bourgeoisie has subjected the country to the rule of the towns. It has created enormous cities, has greatly increased the urban population as compared with the rural, and has thus rescued a considerable part of the population from the idiocy of rural life. Just as it has made the country dependent on the towns, so it has made barbarian and semi-barbarian countries dependent on the civilized ones, nations of peasants on nations of bourgeois, the East on the West.

The bourgeoisie keeps more and more doing away with the scattered state of the population, of the means of production, and of property. It has agglomerated population, centralized the means of production, and has concentrated property in a few hands. The necessary consequence of this was political centralization. Independent, or but loosely connected provinces, with separate interests, laws, governments, and systems of taxation, became lumped together into one nation, with one government, one code of laws, one national class interest, one frontier and one customs tariff.

The bourgeoisie, during its rule of scarce 100 years, has created more massive and more colossal productive forces than have all preceding generations together. Subjection of nature's forces to man, machinery, application of chemistry to industry and agriculture, steam navigation, railways, electric telegraphs, clearing of whole continents for cultivation, canalization of rivers, whole populations conjured out of the ground

— what earlier century had even a presentiment that such productive forces slumbered in the lap of social labor?

We see then: the means of production and of exchange, on whose foundation the bourgeoisie built itself up, were generated in feudal society. At a certain stage in the development of these means of production and of exchange, the conditions under which feudal society produced and exchanged, the feudal organization of agriculture and manufacturing industry, in one word, the feudal relations of property became no longer compatible with the already developed productive forces; they became so many fetters. They had to be burst asunder; they were burst asunder.

Into their place stepped free competition, accompanied by a social and political constitution adapted to it, and by the economic and political sway of the bourgeois class.

A similar movement is going on before our own eyes. Modern bourgeois society, with its relations of production, of exchange and of property, a society that has conjured up such gigantic means of production and of exchange, is like the sorcerer who is no longer able to control the powers of the netherworld whom he has called up by his spells. For many a decade past, the history of industry and commerce is but the history of the revolt of modern productive forces against modern conditions of production, against the property relations that are the conditions for the existence of the bourgeois and of its rule. It is enough to mention the commercial crises that, by their periodical return, put on trial, each time more threateningly, the existence of the entire bourgeois society. In these crises a great part not only of the existing products, but also of the previously created productive forces, are periodically destroyed. In these crises, there breaks out an epidemic that, in all earlier epochs, would have seemed an absurdity — the epidemic of overproduction. Society suddenly finds itself put back into a state of momentary barbarism; it appears as if a famine, a universal war of devastation, had cut off the supply of every means of subsistence; industry and commerce seem to be destroyed. And why?

Because there is too much civilization, too much means of subsistence, too much industry, too much commerce. The productive forces at the disposal of society no longer tend to further the development of the conditions of bourgeois property; on the contrary, they have become too powerful for these conditions, by which they are fettered, and so soon as they overcome these fetters, they bring disorder into the whole of bourgeois society, endanger the existence of bourgeois property. The conditions of bourgeois society are too narrow to comprise the wealth created by them. And how does the bourgeoisie get over these crises? On the one hand, by enforced destruction of a mass of productive forces; on the other, by the conquest of new markets, and by the more thorough exploitation of the old ones. That is to say, by paving the way for more extensive and more destructive crises, and by diminishing the means whereby crises are prevented.

The weapons with which the bourgeoisie felled feudalism to the ground are now turned against the bourgeoisie itself.

But not only has the bourgeoisie forged the weapons that bring death to itself; it has also called into existence the men who are to wield those weapons — the modern working class — the proletarians.

In proportion as the bourgeoisie, i.e., capital, is developed, in the same proportion is the proletariat, the modern working class, developed — a class of laborers, who live only so long as they find work, and who find work only so long as their labor increases capital. These laborers, who must sell themselves piecemeal, are a commodity, like every other article of commerce, and are consequently exposed to all the vicissitudes of competition, to all the fluctuations of the market.

Owing to the extensive use of machinery, and to the division of labor, the work of the proletarians has lost all individual character, and, consequently, all charm for the workman. He becomes an appendage of the machine, and it is only the most simple, most monotonous, and most easily acquired knack, that is required of him. Hence, the cost of production of a workman is restricted, almost entirely, to the means of subsistence that he requires for maintenance, and for the propagation of his race. But the price of a commodity, and therefore also of labor, is equal to its cost of production. In proportion, therefore, as the repulsiveness of the work increases, the wage decreases. What is more, in proportion as the use of machinery and division of labor increases, in the same proportion the burden of toil also increases, whether by prolongation of the working hours, by the increase of the work exacted in a given time, or by increased speed of the machinery, etc.

Modern industry has converted the little workshop of the patriarchal master into the great factory of the industrial capitalist. Masses of laborers, crowded into the factory, are organized like soldiers. As privates of the industrial army, they are placed under the command of a perfect hierarchy of officers and sergeants. Not only are they slaves of the bourgeois class, and of the bourgeois state; they are daily and hourly enslaved by the machine, by the overseer, and, above all, by the individual bourgeois manufacturer himself. The more openly this despotism proclaims gain to be its end and aim, the more petty, the more hateful and the more embittering it is.

The less the skill and exertion of strength implied in manual labor, in other words, the more modern industry becomes developed, the more is the labor of men superseded by that of women. Differences of age and sex have no longer any distinctive social validity for the working class. All are instruments of labor, more or less expensive to use, according to their age and sex.

No sooner is the exploitation of the laborer by the manufacturer so far at an end that he receives his wages in cash, than he is set upon by the other portions of the bourgeoisie, the landlord, the shopkeeper, the pawnbroker, etc.

The lower strata of the middle class — the small tradespeople, shopkeepers, and retired tradesmen generally, the handicraftsmen and peasants — all these sink gradually into the proletariat, partly because their diminutive capital does not suffice for the scale on which modern industry is carried on, and is swamped in the competition with the large capitalists, partly because their specialized skill is rendered worthless by new methods of production. Thus, the proletariat is recruited from all classes of the population.

The proletariat goes through various stages of development. With its birth begins its struggle with the bourgeoisie. At first, the contest is carried on by individual laborers, then by the workpeople of a factory, then by the operatives of one trade, in one locality, against the individual bourgeois who directly exploits them. They direct their attacks not against the bourgeois condition of production, but against the instruments of production themselves; they destroy imported wares that compete with their labor, they smash to pieces machinery, they set factories ablaze, they seek to restore by force the vanished status of the workman of the Middle Ages.

At this stage, the laborers still form an incoherent mass scattered over the whole country, and broken up by their mutual competition. If anywhere they unite to form more compact bodies, this is not yet the consequence of their own active union, but of the union of the bourgeoisie, which class, in order to attain its own political ends, is compelled to set the whole proletariat in motion, and is moreover yet, for a time, able to do so. At this stage, therefore, the proletarians do not fight their enemies, but the enemies of their enemies, the remnants of absolute monarchy, the landowners, the nonindustrial bourgeois, the petty bourgeoisie. Thus, the whole historical movement is concentrated in the hands of the bourgeoisie; every victory so obtained is a victory for the bourgeoisie.

But with the development of industry the proletariat not only increases in number; it becomes concentrated in greater masses, its strength grows, and it feels that strength more. The various interests and conditions of life within the ranks of the proletariat are more and more equalized, in proportion as machinery obliterates all distinctions of labor, and nearly everywhere reduces wages to the same low level. The growing competition among the bourgeois, and the resulting commercial crises, make the wages of the workers ever more fluctuating. The unceasing improvement of machinery, ever more rapidly developing, makes their livelihood more and more precarious; the collisions between individual workmen and individual bourgeois take more and more the character of collisions between two classes. Thereupon, the workers begin to form combinations (trade unions) against the bourgeois; they club together in order to keep up the rate of wages; they found permanent associations in order to make provision beforehand for these occasional revolts. Here and there the contest breaks out into riots.

Now and then the workers are victorious, but only for a time. The real fruit of their battles lies not in the immediate result, but in the ever expanding union of the workers. This union is helped on by the improved means of communication that are created by modern industry, and that place the workers of different localities in contact with one another. It was just this contact that was needed to centralize the numerous local struggles, all of the same character, into one national struggle between classes. But every class struggle is a political struggle. And that union, to attain which the burghers of the Middle Ages, with their miserable highways, required centuries, the modern proletarians, thanks to railways, achieve in a few years.

This organization of the proletarians into a class, and consequently into a political party, is continually being upset again by the competition between the workers themselves. But it ever rises up again, stronger, firmer, mightier. It compels legislative recognition of particular interests of the workers, by taking advantage of the divisions among the bourgeoisie itself. Thus, the Ten Hours Bill in England was carried.

Altogether, collisions between the classes of the old society further in many ways the course of development of the proletariat. The bourgeoisie finds itself involved in a constant battle: at first with the aristocracy; later on, with those portions of the bourgeoisie itself, whose interests have become antagonistic to the progress of industry; at all times with the bourgeoisie of foreign countries. In all these battles, it sees itself compelled to appeal to the proletariat, to ask for its help, and thus to drag it into the political arena. The bourgeoisie itself, therefore, supplies the proletariat with its own elements of political and general education, in other words, it furnishes the proletariat with weapons for fighting the bourgeoisie.

Further, as we have already seen, entire sections of the ruling classes are, by the advance of industry, precipitated into the proletariat, or are at least threatened in their conditions of existence. These also supply the proletariat with fresh elements of enlightenment and progress.

Finally, in times when the class struggle nears the decisive hour, the progress of dissolution going on within the ruling class, in fact within the whole range of old society, assumes such a violent, glaring character, that a small section of the ruling class cuts itself adrift, and joins the revolutionary class, the class that holds the future in its hands. Just as, therefore, at an earlier period, a section of the nobility went over to the bourgeoisie, so now a portion of the bourgeoisie goes over to the proletariat, and in particular, a portion of the bourgeois ideologists, who have raised themselves to the level of comprehending theoretically the historical movement as a whole.

Of all the classes that stand face to face with the bourgeoisie today, the proletariat alone is a genuinely revolutionary class. The other classes decay and finally disappear in the face of modern industry; the proletariat is its special and essential product.

The lower middle class, the small manufacturer, the shopkeeper, the artisan, the peasant, all these fight against the bourgeoisie, to save from extinction their existence as fractions of the middle class. They are therefore not revolutionary, but conservative. Nay, more, they are reactionary, for they try to roll back the wheel of history. If by chance they are revolutionary, they are only so in view of their impending transfer into the proletariat; they thus defend not their present, but their future interests; they desert their own standpoint to place themselves at that of the proletariat.

The "dangerous class," the social scum, that passively rotting mass thrown off by the lowest layers of the old society, may, here and there, be swept into the movement by a proletarian revolution; its conditions of life, however, prepare it far more for the part of a bribed tool of reactionary intrigue.

In the conditions of the proletariat, those of old society at large are already virtually swamped. The proletarian is without property; his relation to his wife and children has no longer anything in common with the bourgeois family relations; modern industrial labor, modern subjection to capital, the same in England as in France, in America as in Germany, has stripped him of every trace of national character. Law, morality, religion, are to him so many bourgeois prejudices, behind which lurk in ambush just as many bourgeois interests.

All the preceding classes that got the upper hand sought to fortify their already acquired status by subjecting society at large to their conditions of appropriation. The proletarians cannot become masters of the productive forces of society, except by abolishing their own previous mode of appropriation, and thereby also every other previous mode of appropriation. They have nothing of their own to secure and to fortify; their mission is to destroy all previous securities for, and insurances of, individual property.

All previous historical movements were movements of minorities, or in the interest of minorities. The proletarian movement is the self-conscious, independent movement of the immense majority, in the interest of the immense majority. The proletariat, the lowest stratum of our present society, cannot stir, cannot raise itself up, without the whole superincumbent strata of official society being sprung into the air.

Though not in substance, yet in form, the struggle of the proletariat with the bourgeoisie is at first a national struggle. The proletariat of each country must, of course, first of all settle matters with its own bourgeoisie.

In depicting the most general phases of the development of the proletariat, we traced the more or less veiled civil war, raging within existing society, up to the point where that war breaks out into open revolution, and where the violent overthrow of the bourgeoisie lays the foundation for the sway of the proletariat.

Hitherto, every form of society has been based, as we have already seen, on the antagonism of oppressing and oppressed classes. But in order to oppress a class, certain conditions must be assured to it under which it can, at least, continue its slavish existence. The serf, in the period of serfdom, raised himself to membership in the commune, just as the petty bourgeois, under the yoke of the feudal absolutism, managed to develop into a bourgeois. The modern laborer, on the contrary, instead of rising with the progress of industry, sinks deeper and deeper below the conditions of existence of his own class. He becomes a pauper, and pauperism develops more rapidly than population and wealth. And here it becomes evident that the bourgeoisie is unfit any longer to be the ruling class in society, and to impose its conditions of existence upon society as an overriding law. It is unfit to rule because it is incompetent to assure an existence to its slave within his slavery, because it cannot help letting him sink into such a state that it has to feed him, instead of being fed by him. Society can no longer live under this bourgeoisie, in other words, its existence is no longer compatible with society.

The essential conditions for the existence, and for the sway of the bourgeois class, is the formation and augmentation of capital; the condition for capital is wage labor. Wage labor rests exclusively on competition between the laborers. The advance of industry, whose involuntary promoter is the bourgeoisie, replaces the isolation of the laborers, due to competition, by their revolutionary combination, due to association. The development of modern industry, therefore, cuts from under its feet the very foundation on which the bourgeoisie produces and appropriates products. What the bourgeoisie therefore produces, above all, are its own grave-diggers. Its fall and the victory of the proletariat are equally inevitable.

II. PROLETARIANS AND COMMUNISTS

In what relation do the Communists stand to the proletarians as a whole? The Communists do not form a separate party opposed to the other working-class parties.

They have no interests separate and apart from those of the proletariat as a whole.

They do not set up any sectarian principles of their own, by which to shape and mold the proletarian movement.

The Communists are distinguished from the other working-class parties by this only:

1. In the national struggles of the proletarians of the different countries, they point out and bring to the front the common interests of the entire proletariat, independently of all nationality.

2. In the various stages of development which the struggle of the working class against the bourgeoisie has to pass through, they always and everywhere represent the interests of the movement as a whole.

The Communists, therefore, are on the one hand, practically, the most advanced and resolute section of the working-class parties of every country, that section which pushes forward all others; on the other hand, theoretically, they have over the great mass of the proletariat the advantage of clearly understanding the line of march, the conditions, and the ultimate general results of the proletarian movement.

The immediate aim of the Communists is the same as that of all the other proletarian parties: Formation of the proletariat into a class, overthrow of the bourgeois supremacy, conquest of political power by the proletariat.

The theoretical conclusions of the Communists are in no way based on ideas or principles that have been invented, or discovered, by this or that would-be universal reformer.

They merely express, in general terms, actual relations springing from an existing class struggle, from a historical movement going on under our very eyes. The abolition of existing property relations is not at all a distinctive feature of communism.

All property relations in the past have continually been subject to historical change consequent upon the change in historical conditions.

The French Revolution, for example, abolished feudal property in favor of bourgeois property.

The distinguishing feature of communism is not the abolition of property generally, but the abolition of bourgeois property. But modern bourgeois private property is the final and most complete expression of the system of producing and appropriating products that is based on class antagonisms, on the exploitation of the many by the few.

In this sense, the theory of the Communists may be summed up in the single sentence: Abolition of private property.

We Communists have been reproached with the desire of abolishing the right of personally acquiring property as the fruit of a man's own labor, which property is alleged to be the groundwork of all personal freedom, activity and independence.

Hard-won, self-acquired, self-earned property! Do you mean the property of petty artisan and of the small peasant, a form of property that preceded the bourgeois form? There is no need to abolish that; the development of industry has to a great extent already destroyed it, and is still destroying it daily.

Or do you mean the modern bourgeois private property?

But does wage labor create any property for the laborer? Not a bit. It creates capital, i.e., that kind of property which exploits wage labor, and which cannot increase except upon conditions of begetting a new supply of wage labor for fresh exploitation. Property, in its present form, is based on the antagonism of capital and wage labor. Let us examine both sides of this antagonism.

To be a capitalist, is to have not only a purely personal, but a social status in production. Capital is a collective product, and only by the united action of many members, nay, in the last resort, only by the united action of all members of society, can it be set in motion.

Capital is therefore not a personal, it is a social power.

When, therefore, capital is converted into common property, into the property of all members of society, personal property is not thereby transformed into social property. It is only the social character of the property that is changed. It loses its class character.

Let us now take wage labor.

The average price of wage labor is the minimum wage, i.e., that quantum of the means of subsistence which is absolutely requisite to keep the laborer in bare existence as a laborer. What, therefore, the wage laborer appropriates by means of his labor, merely suffices to prolong and reproduce a bare existence. We by no means intend to abolish this personal appropriation of the products of labor, an appropriation that is made for the maintenance and reproduction of human life, and that leaves no surplus wherewith to command the labor of others. All that we want to do away with is the miserable character of this appropriation, under which the laborer lives merely to increase capital, and is allowed to live only in so far as the interest of the ruling class requires it.

In bourgeois society, living labor is but a means to increase accumulated labor. In communist society, accumulated labor is but a means to widen, to enrich, to promote the existence of the laborer.

In bourgeois society, therefore, the past dominates the present; in communist society, the present dominates the past. In bourgeois society, capital is independent and has individuality, while the living person is dependent and has no individuality.

And the abolition of this state of things is called by the bourgeois, abolition of individuality and freedom! And rightly so. The abolition of bourgeois individuality, bourgeois independence, and bourgeois freedom is undoubtedly aimed at.

By freedom is meant, under the present bourgeois conditions of production, free trade, free selling and buying.

But if selling and buying disappears, free selling and buying disappears also. This talk about free selling and buying, and all the other "brave words" of our bourgeoisie about freedom in general, have a meaning, if any, only in contrast with restricted selling and buying, with the fettered traders of the Middle Ages, but have no meaning when opposed to the communistic abolition of buying and selling, of the bourgeois conditions of production, and the bourgeoisie itself.

You are horrified at our intending to do away with private property. But in your existing society, private property is already done away with for nine-tenths of the population; its existence for the few is solely due to its nonexistence in the hands of those nine-tenths. You reproach us, therefore, with intending to do away with a form of property, the necessary condition for whose existence is the non-existence of any property for the immense majority of society.

In one word, you reproach us with intending to do away with your property. Precisely so; that is just what we intend.

From the moment when labor can no longer be converted into capital, money, or rent, into a social power capable of being monopolized, i.e., from the moment when individual property can no longer be transformed into bourgeois property, into capital, from that moment, you say, individuality vanishes.

You must, therefore, confess that by "individual" you mean no other person than the bourgeois, than the middle-class owner of property. This person must, indeed, be swept out of the way, and made impossible.

Communism deprives no man of the power to appropriate the products of society; all that it does is to deprive him of the power to subjugate the labor of others by means of such appropriation.

It has been objected that upon the abolition of private property all work will cease, and universal laziness will overtake us.

According to this, bourgeois society ought long ago to have gone to the dogs through sheer idleness; for those of its members who work, acquire nothing, and those who acquire anything, do not work. The whole of this objection is but another expression of the tautology: that there can no longer be any wage labor when there is no longer any capital.

All objections urged against the communistic mode of producing and appropriating material products have, in the same way, been urged against the communistic mode of producing and appropriating intellectual products. Just as, to the bourgeois, the disappearance of

class property is the disappearance of production itself, so the disappearance of class culture is to him identical with the disappearance of
all culture.

That culture, the loss of which he laments, is, for the enormous
majority, a mere training to act as a machine.

But don't wrangle with us so long as you apply, to our intended
abolition of bourgeois property, the standard of your bourgeois notions
of freedom, culture, law, etc. Your very ideas are but the out-growth of
the conditions of your bourgeois production and bourgeois property,
just as your jurisprudence is but the will of your class made into a law
for all, a will whose essential character and direction are determined
by the economical conditions of existence of your class.

The selfish misconception that induces you to transform into eternal
laws of nature and of reason the social forms springing from your present mode of production and form of property — historical relations that
rise and disappear in the progress of production — this misconception
you share with every ruling class that has preceded you. What you see
clearly in the case of ancient property, what you admit in the case of
feudal property, you are of course forbidden to admit in the case of
your own bourgeois form of property.

Abolition of the family! Even the most radical flare up at this in-
famous proposal of the Communists.

On what foundation is the present family, the bourgeois family,
based? On capital, on private gain. In its completely developed form,
this family exists only among the bourgeoisie. But this state of things
finds its complement in the practical absence of the family among proletarians, and in public prostitution.

The bourgeois family will vanish as a matter of course when its
complement vanishes, and both will vanish with the vanishing of
capital.

Do you charge us with wanting to stop the exploitation of children
by their parents? To this crime we plead guilty.

But, you will say, we destroy the most hallowed of relations, when we replace home education by social.

And your education! Is not that also social, and determined by the social conditions under which you educate, by the intervention direct or indirect, of society, by means of schools, etc.? The Communists have not intended the intervention of society in education; they do but seek to alter the character of that intervention, and to rescue education from the influence of the ruling class.

The bourgeois claptrap about the family and education, about the hallowed co-relation of parents and child, becomes all the more disgusting, the more, by the action of modern industry, all family ties among the proletarians are torn asunder, and their children transformed into simple articles of commerce and instruments of labor.

But you Communists would introduce community of women, screams the whole bourgeoisie in chorus.

The bourgeois sees in his wife a mere instrument of production. He hears that the instruments of production are to be exploited in common, and, naturally, can come to no other conclusion than the lot of being common to all will likewise fall to the women.

He has not even a suspicion that the real point aimed at is to do away with the status of women as mere instruments of production.

For the rest, nothing is more ridiculous than the virtuous indignation of our bourgeois at the community of women which, they pretend, is to be openly and officially established by the Communists. The Communists have no need to introduce community of women; it has existed almost from time immemorial.

Our bourgeois, not content with having wives and daughters of their proletarians at their disposal, not to speak of common prostitutes, take the greatest pleasure in seducing each other's wives.

Bourgeois marriage is in reality a system of wives in common and thus, at the most, what the Communists might possibly be reproached with is that they desire to introduce, in substitution for a hypocritically concealed, an openly legalized community of women. For the rest, it is self-evident that the abolition of the present system of production must bring with it the abolition of the community of women springing from that system, i.e., of prostitution both public and private.

The Communists are further reproached with desiring to abolish countries and nationality.

The working men have no country. We cannot take from them what they have not got. Since the proletariat must first of all acquire political supremacy, must rise to be the leading class of the nation, must constitute itself as the nation, it is, so far, itself national, though not in the bourgeois sense of the word.

National differences and antagonism between peoples are daily more and more vanishing, owing to the development of the bourgeoisie, to freedom of commerce, to the world market, to uniformity in the mode of production and in the conditions of life corresponding thereto.

The supremacy of the proletariat will cause them to vanish still faster. United action, of the leading civilized countries at least, is one of the first conditions for the emancipation of the proletariat.

In proportion as the exploitation of one individual by another is put an end to, the exploitation of one nation by another will also be put an end to. In proportion as the antagonism between classes within the nation vanishes, the hostility of one nation to another will come to an end.

The charges against communism made from a religious, a philosophical and, generally, from an ideological standpoint, are not deserving of serious examination.

Does it require deep intuition to comprehend that man's ideas, views, and conceptions, in one word, man's consciousness, changes with every change in the conditions of his material existence, in his social relations and in his social life?

What else does the history of ideas prove, than that intellectual production changes its character in proportion as material production is changed? The ruling ideas of each age have ever been the ideas of its ruling class.

When people speak of the ideas that revolutionize society, they do but express that fact that within the old society the elements of a new one have been created, and that the dissolution of the old ideas keeps even pace with the dissolution of the old conditions of existence.

When the ancient world was in its last throes, the ancient religions were overcome by Christianity. When Christian ideas succumbed in the 18th century to rationalist ideas, feudal society fought its death battle with the then revolutionary bourgeoisie. The ideas of religious liberty and freedom of conscience merely gave expression to the sway of free competition within the domain of knowledge.

"Undoubtedly," it will be said, "religious, moral, philosophical and juridicial ideas have been modified in the course of historical development. But religion, morality, philosophy, political science and law constantly survived this change."

"There are, besides, eternal truths, such as freedom, justice, etc., that are common to all states of society. But communism abolishes eternal truths, it abolishes all religion and all morality, instead of constituting them on a new basis; it therefore acts in contradiction to all past historical experience."

What does this accusation reduce itself to? The history of all past society has consisted in the development of class antagonisms, antagonisms that assumed different forms at different epochs.

But whatever form they may have taken, one fact is common to all past ages, viz., the exploitation of one part of society by the other. No wonder, then, that the social consciousness of past ages, despite all the multiplicity and variety it displays, moves within certain common forms, or general ideas, which cannot completely vanish except with the total disappearance of class antagonisms.

The communist revolution is the most radical rupture with traditional property relations; no wonder that its development involves the most radical rupture with traditional ideas.

But let us have done with the bourgeois objections to communism.

We have seen above that the first step in the revolution by the working class is to raise the proletariat to the position of ruling class, to win the battle of democracy.

The proletariat will use its political supremacy to wrest, by degrees, all capital from the bourgeoisie, to centralize all instruments of production in the hands of the state, i.e., of the proletariat organized as the ruling class, and to increase the total productive forces as rapidly as possible.

Of course, in the beginning, this cannot be effected except by means of despotic inroads on the rights of property, and on the conditions of bourgeois production; by means of measures, therefore, which appear economically insufficient and untenable, but which, in the course of the movement, outstrip themselves, necessitate further inroads upon the old social order, and are unavoidable as a means of entirely revolutionizing the mode of production.

These measures will, of course, be different in different countries.

Nevertheless, in most advanced countries, the following will be pretty generally applicable.

1. Abolition of property in land and application of all rents of land to public purposes.

2. A heavy progressive or graduated income tax.

3. Abolition of all rights of inheritance.

4. Confiscation of the property of all emigrants and rebels.

5. Centralization of credit in the hands of the state, by means of a national bank with state capital and an exclusive monopoly.

6. Centralization of the means of communication and transport in the hands of the state.

7. Extension of factories and instruments of production owned by the state; the bringing into cultivation of waste lands, and the improvement of the soil generally in accordance with a common plan.

8. Equal obligation of all to labor. Establishment of industrial armies, especially for agriculture.

9. Combination of agriculture with manufacturing industries; gradual

abolition of the distinction between town and country, by a more equable distribution of the populace over the country.

10. Free education for all children in public schools. Abolition of children's factory labor in its present form. Combination of education with industrial production, etc.

When, in the course of development, class distinctions have disappeared, and all production has been concentrated in the hands of a vast association of the whole nation, the public power will lose its political character. Political power, properly so called, is merely the organized power of one class for oppressing another. If the proletariat during its contest with the bourgeoisie is compelled, by the force of circumstances, to organize itself as a class; if, by means of a revolution, it makes itself the ruling class, and, as such, sweeps away by force the old conditions of production, then it will, along with these conditions, have swept away the conditions for the existence of class antagonisms and of classes generally, and will thereby have abolished its own supremacy as a class.

In place of the old bourgeois society, with its classes and class antagonisms, we shall have an association in which the free development of each is the condition for the free development of all.

III. SOCIALIST AND COMMUNIST LITERATURE

1. Reactionary Socialism

a. Feudal Socialism.　　Owing to their historical position, it became the vocation of the aristocracies of France and England to write pamphlets against modern bourgeois society. In the French Revolution of July 1830, and in the English Reform agitation, these aristocracies again succumbed to the hateful upstart. Thenceforth, a serious political struggle was altogether out of the question. A literary battle alone remained possible. But even in the domain of literature the old cries of the Restoration period had become impossible.[5]

In order to arouse sympathy, the aristocracy were obliged to lose sight, apparently, of their own interests, and to formulate their indictment against the bourgeoisie in the interest of the exploited working class alone. Thus, the aristocracy took their revenge by singing lampoons on their new master and whispering in his ears sinister prophecies of coming catastrophe.

In this way arose feudal socialism: half lamentation, half lampoon; half an echo of the past, half menace of the future; at times, by its bitter, witty and incisive criticism, striking the bourgeoisie to the very heart's core, but always ludicrous in its effect, through total incapacity to comprehend the march of modern history.

The aristocracy, in order to rally the people to them, waved the proletarian alms-bag in front for a banner. But the people, so often as it joined them, saw on their hindquarters the old feudal coats of arms, and deserted with loud and irreverent laughter.

One section of the French Legitimists and "Young England" exhibited this spectacle.

In pointing out that their mode of exploitation was different to that of the bourgeoisie, the feudalists forget that they exploited under circumstances and conditions that were quite different and that are now antiquated. In showing that, under their rule, the modern proletariat never existed, they forget that the modern bourgeoisie is the necessary offspring of their own form of society.

For the rest, so little do they conceal the reactionary character of their criticism that their chief accusation against the bourgeoisie amounts to this: that under the bourgeois regime a class is being developed which is destined to cut up, root and branch, the old order of society.

What they upbraid the bourgeoisie with is not so much that it creates a proletariat, as that it creates a *revolutionary* proletariat.

In political practice, therefore, they join in all corrective measures against the working class; and in ordinary life, despite their highfalutin phrases, they stoop to pick up the golden apples dropped from the tree of industry, and to barter truth, love, and honor for traffic in wool, beetroot-sugar, and potato spirits.[6]

As the parson has ever gone hand in hand with the landlord, so has clerical socialism with feudal socialism.

Nothing is easier than to give Christian asceticism a socialist tinge. Has not Christianity declaimed against private property, against marriage, against the state? Has it not preached in the place of these, charity and poverty, celibacy and mortification of the flesh, monastic life and Mother Church? Christian socialism is but the holy water with which the priest consecrates the heartburnings of the aristocrat.

b. Petty-Bourgeois Socialism.   The feudal aristocracy was not the only class that was ruined by the bourgeoisie, not the only class whose conditions of existence pined and perished in the atmosphere of modern bourgeois society. The medieval burgesses and the small peasant proprietors were the precursors of the modern bourgeoisie. In those countries which are but little developed, industrially and commercially, these two classes still vegetate side by side with the rising bourgeoisie.

In countries where modern civilization has become fully developed, a new class of petty bourgeois has been formed, fluctuating between proletariat and bourgeoisie and ever renewing itself a supplementary part of bourgeois society. The individual members of this class, however, are being constantly hurled down into the proletariat by the action of competition, and, as modern industry develops, they even see the moment approaching when they will completely disappear as an independent section of modern society, to be replaced in manufacture, agriculture and commerce, by over-seers, bailiffs and shop assistants.

In countries like France, where the peasants constitute far more than half of the population, it was natural that writers who sided with the proletariat against the bourgeoisie should use, in their criticism of the bourgeois regime, the standard of the peasant and petty bourgeois, and from the standpoint of these intermediate classes should take up the cudgels for the working class. Thus arose petty-bourgeois socialism. Sismondi was the head of this school, not only in France but also in England.

This school of socialism dissected with great acuteness the contra-dictions in the conditions of modern production. It laid bare the hypocritical apologies of economists. It proved, incontrovertibly, the disastrous effects of machinery and division of labor; the concentra-tion of capital and land in a few hands; overproduction and crises; it pointed out the inevitable ruin of the petty bourgeois and peasant, the misery of the proletariat, the anarchy in production, the crying inequalities in the distribution of wealth, the industrial war of exter-mination between nations, the dissolution of old moral bonds, of the old family relations, of the old nationalities.

In its positive aims, however, this form of socialism aspires either to restoring the old means of production and of exchange, and with them the old property relations and the old society, or to cramping the modern means of production and of exchange within the frame-work of the old property relations that have been, and were bound to be, exploded by those means. In either case, it is both reactionary and utopian.

Its last words are: corporate guilds for manufacture; patriarchal relations in agriculture.

Ultimately, when stubborn historical facts had dispersed all in-toxicating effects of self-deception, this form of socialism ended in a miserable fit of the blues.

c. German or "True" Socialism. The socialist and communist literature of France, a literature that originated under the pressure of a bour-geoisie in power, and that was the expression of the struggle against this power, was introduced into Germany at a time when the bour-geoisie in that country had just begun its contest with feudal absol-utism.

German philosophers, would-be philosophers, and *beaux esprits* (men of letters), eagerly seized on this literature, only forgetting that when these writings immigrated from France into Germany, French social conditions had not immigrated along with them. In contact with

German social conditions, this French literature lost all its imme-diate practical significance and assumed a purely literary aspect. Thus, to the German philosophers of the 18th century, the demands of the first French Revolution were nothing more than the demands of "practical reason" in general, and the utterance of the will of the revolutionary French bourgeoisie signified, in their eyes, the laws of pure will, of will as it was bound to be, of true human will generally.

The work of the German *literati* consisted solely in bringing the new French ideas into harmony with their ancient philosophical conscience, or rather, in annexing the French ideas without deserting their own philosophic point of view.

This annexation took place in the same way in which a foreign language is appropriated, namely, by translation.

It is well known how the monks wrote silly lives of Catholic saints *over* the manuscripts on which the classical works of ancient heathen-dom had been written. The German *literati* reversed this pro-cess with the profane French literature. They wrote their philosophi-cal nonsense beneath the French original. For instance, beneath the French criticism of the economic functions of money, they wrote "alienation of human-ity," and beneath the French criticism of the bourgeois state they wrote, "dethronement of the category of the general," and so forth.

The introduction of these philosophical phrases at the back of the French historical criticisms, they dubbed "philosophy of action," "true socialism," "German science of socialism," "philosophical foundation of socialism," and so on.

The French socialist and communist literature was thus com-pletely emasculated. And, since it ceased, in the hands of the German to express the struggle of one class with the other, he felt conscious of having overcome "French one-sidedness" and of representing, not true requirements, but the requirements of truth; not the interests of the proletariat, but the interests of human nature, of man in general, who belongs to no class, has no reality, who exists only in the misty realm of philosophical fantasy.

This German socialism, which took its schoolboy task so seriously and solemnly, and extolled its poor stock-in-trade in such mounte-bank fashion, meanwhile gradually lost its pedantic innocence.

The fight of the German, and especially the Prussian bourgeoisie, against feudal aristocracy and absolute monarchy, in other words, the liberal movement, became more earnest.

By this, the long-wished-for opportunity was offered to "true" socialism of confronting the political movement with the socialistic demands, of hurling the traditional anathemas against liberalism, against representative government, against bourgeois competition, bourgeois freedom of the press, bourgeois legislation, bourgeois liberty and equality, and of preaching to the masses that they had nothing to gain, and everything to lose, by this bourgeois movement. German socialism forgot, in the nick of time, that the French criticism, whose silly echo it was, presupposed the existence of modern bour-geois society, with its corresponding economic conditions of exis-tence, and the political constitution adapted thereto, the very things whose attainment was the object of the pending struggle in Germany.

To the absolute governments, with their following of parsons, professors, country squires and officials, it served as a welcome scare-crow against the threatening bourgeoisie.

It was a sweet finish, after the bitter pills of flogging and bullets with which these same governments, just at that time, dosed the German working-class risings.

While this "true" socialism thus served the government as a weapon for fighting the German bourgeoisie, it, at the same time, directly represented a reactionary interest, the interest of German philistines. In Germany, the petty-bourgeois class, a relic of the 16th century, and since then constantly cropping up again under various forms, is the real social basis of the existing state of things.

To preserve this class is to preserve the existing state of things in Germany. The industrial and political supremacy of the bourgeoisie threatens it with certain destruction — on the one hand, from the concentration of capital; on the other, from the rise of a revolutionary proletariat. "True" socialism appeared to kill these two birds with one stone. It spread like an epidemic.

The robe of speculative cobwebs, embroidered with flowers of rhetoric, steeped in the dew of sickly sentiment, this transcendental robe in which the German socialists wrapped their sorry "eternal truths," all skin and bone, served to wonderfully increase the sale of their goods amongst such a public.

And on its part, German socialism recognized, more and more, its own calling as the bombastic representative of the petty-bourgeois philistine.

It proclaimed the German nation to be the model nation, and the German petty philistine to be the typical man. To every villainous meanness of this model man, it gave a hidden, higher, socialistic interpretation, the exact contrary of its real character. It went to the extreme length of directly opposing the "brutally destructive" tenden-cy of communism, and of proclaiming its supreme and impartial contempt of all class struggles. With very few exceptions, all the so-called socialist and communist publications that now (1847) circu-late in Germany belong to the domain of this foul and enervating literature.[7]

2. Conservative or Bourgeois Socialism

A part of the bourgeoisie is desirous of redressing social grievances in order to secure the continued existence of bourgeois society.

To this section belong economists, philanthropists, humanitar-ians, improvers of the condition of the working class, organizers of charity, members of societies for the prevention of cruelty to animals, temperance fanatics, hole-and-corner reformers of every imaginable kind. This form of socialism has, moreover, been worked out into complete systems.

We may cite Proudhon's *Philosophie de la Misère* (*The Philosophy of Poverty*) as an example of this form.

The socialistic bourgeois want all the advantages of modern soc-ial conditions without the struggles and dangers necessarily result-ing therefrom. They desire the existing state of society minus its rev-olutionary and disintegrating elements. They wish for a bourgeoisie without a proletariat. The bourgeoisie naturally conceives the world in which it is supreme to be the best; and bourgeois socialism dev-elops this comfortable conception into various more or less complete systems. In requiring the proletariat to carry out such a system, and thereby to march straightway into the social New Jerusalem, it but requires in reality that the proletariat should remain within the bounds of exist-ing society, but should cast away all its hateful ideas concerning the bourgeoisie.

A second and more practical, but less systematic, form of this social-ism sought to depreciate every revolutionary movement in the eyes of the working class by showing that no mere political reform, but only a change in the material conditions of existence, in economi-cal rela-tions, could be of any advantage to them. By changes in the material conditions of existence, this form of socialism, however, by no means understands abolition of the bourgeois relations of produc-tion, an abolition that can be affected only by a revolution, but admin-istrative reforms, based on the continued existence of these relations; reforms, therefore, that in no respect affect the relations between capital and labor, but, at the best, lessen the cost, and simplify the administrative work of bourgeois government.

Bourgeois socialism attains adequate expression when, and only when, it becomes a mere figure of speech.

Free trade: for the benefit of the working class. Protective duties: for the benefit of the working class. Prison reform: for the benefit of the working class. This is the last word and the only seriously meant word of bourgeois socialism.

It is summed up in the phrase: the bourgeois is a bourgeois — for the benefit of the working class.

3. Critical-Utopian Socialism and Communism

We do not here refer to that literature which, in every great modern revolution, has always given voice to the demands of the proletariat, such as the writings of Babeuf and others.

The first direct attempts of the proletariat to attain its own ends, made in times of universal excitement, when feudal society was being overthrown, these attempts necessarily failed, owing to the then undeveloped state of the proletariat, as well as to the absence of the economic conditions for its emancipation, conditions that had yet to be produced, and could be produced by the impending bour-geois epoch alone. The revolutionary literature that accompanied these first movements of the proletariat had necessarily a reactionary character. It inculcated universal asceticism and social levelling in its crudest form.

The socialist and communist systems properly so-called, those of Saint-Simon, Fourier, Owen and others, spring into existence in the early undeveloped period, described above, of the struggle bet-ween proletariat and bourgeoisie (see Section I. Bourgeois and Prole-tarians).

The founders of these systems see, indeed, the class antagonisms, as well as the action of the decomposing elements in the prevailing form of society. But the proletariat, as yet in its infancy, offers to them the spectacle of a class without any historical initiative or any independent political movement.

Since the development of class antagonism keeps even pace with the development of industry, the economic situation, as they find it, does not as yet offer to them the material conditions for the emancipa-tion of the proletariat. They therefore search after a new social science, after new social laws, that are to create these conditions.

Historical action is to yield to their personal inventive action; historically created conditions of emancipation to fantastic ones, and the gradual, spontaneous class organization of the proletariat to an organization of society especially contrived by these inventors. Future history resolves itself, in their eyes, into the propaganda and the practical carrying out of their social plans.

In the formation of their plans, they are conscious of caring chiefly for the interests of the working class, as being the most suffering class. Only from the point of view of being the most suffering class does the proletariat exist for them.

The undeveloped state of the class struggle, as well as their own surroundings, cause socialists of this kind to consider themselves far superior to all class antagonisms. They want to improve the con-dition of every member of society, even that of the most favored. Hence, they habitually appeal to society at large, without the distinc-tion of class; nay, by preference, to the ruling class. For how can people, when once they understand their system, fail to see in it the best possible plan of the best possible state of society?

Hence, they reject all political, and especially all revolutionary ac-tion; they wish to attain their ends by peaceful means, and endeav-or, by small experiments, necessarily doomed to failure, and by the force of example, to pave the way for the new social gospel.

Such fantastic pictures of future society, painted at a time when the proletariat is still in a very undeveloped state and has but a fan-tastic conception of its own position, correspond with the first instinc-tive yearnings of that class for a general reconstruction of society.

But these socialist and communist publications contain also a critical element. They attack every principle of existing society. Hence, they are full of the most valuable materials for the enlightenment of the working class. The practical measures proposed in them — such as the abolition of the distinction between town and country, of the family, of the carrying on of industries for the account of private individu-als, and of the wage system, the proclamation of social har-mony, the conversion of the function of the state into a mere super-intendence of production — all these proposals point solely to the disappearance of class antagonisms which were, at that time, only just cropping up, and which, in these publications, are recognized in their earliest, indistinct and undefined forms only. These propo-sals, therefore, are of a purely utopian character.

The significance of critical-utopian socialism and communism bears an inverse relation to historical development. In proportion as the modern class struggle develops and takes definite shape, this fantastic standing apart from the contest, these fantastic attacks on it, lose all practical value and all theoretical justification. Therefore, although the originators of these systems were, in many respects, revolutionary, their disciples have, in every case, formed mere reac-tionary sects. They hold fast by the original views of their masters, in opposition to the progressive historical development of the prol-etariat. They therefore endeavor, and that consistently, to deaden the class struggle and to reconcile the class antagonisms. They still dream of experimental realization of their social utopias, of founding isolated *phalanstères*, of establishing "home colonies," or setting up a "little Icaria"[8] — duodecimo editions of the New Jerusalem — and to realize all these castles in the air, they are compelled to appeal to the feelings and purses of the bourgeois. By degrees, they sink into the category of the reactionary conservative socialists depicted above, differing from these only by more systematic pedantry, and by their fanatical and superstitious belief in the miraculous effects of their social science.

They therefore violently oppose all political action on the part of the working class; such action, according to them, can only result from blind unbelief in the new gospel.

The Owenites in England, and the Fourierists in France, respectively, oppose the Chartists and the Réformistes.

IV. POSITION OF THE COMMUNISTS IN RELATION TO THE VARIOUS EXISTING OPPOSITION PARTIES

Section II has made clear the relations of the Communists to the exis-ting working-class parties, such as the Chartists in England and the agrarian reformers in America.

The Communists fight for the attainment of the immediate aims, for the enforcement of the momentary interests of the working class; but in the movement of the present, they also represent and take care of the future of that movement. In France the Communists ally with the Social Democrats,[9] against the conservative and radical bour-geoisie, reserv-ing, however, the right to take up a critical position in regard to phases and illusions traditionally handed down from the great Revolution.

In Switzerland they support the Radicals, without losing sight of the fact that this party consists of antagonistic elements, partly of democratic socialists, in the French sense, partly of radical bourgeois.

In Poland they support the party that insists on an agrarian revol-ution as the prime condition for national emancipation, that party which fomented the insurrection of Cracow in 1846.

In Germany they fight with the bourgeoisie whenever it acts in a revolutionary way, against the absolute monarchy, the feudal squire-archy, and the petty-bourgeoisie.

But they never cease, for a single instant, to instil into the working class the clearest possible recognition of the hostile antagonism bet-ween bourgeoisie and proletariat, in order that the German workers may straightway use, as so many weapons against the bourgeoisie, the social and political conditions that the bourgeoisie must neces-sarily introduce along with its supremacy, and in order that, after the fall of the reactionary classes in Germany, the fight against the bourgeoisie itself may immediately begin.

The Communists turn their attention chiefly to Germany, because that country is on the eve of a bourgeois revolution that is bound to be carried out under more advanced conditions of European civiliza-tion, and with a much more developed proletariat than that of England was in the 17th, and France in the 18th century, and because the bourgeois revolution in Germany will be but the prelude to an immediately following proletarian revolution.

In short, the Communists everywhere support every revolution-ary movement against the existing social and political order of things.

In all these movements, they bring to the front, as the leading question in each, the property question, no matter what its degree of development at the time.

Finally, they labor everywhere for the union and agreement of the democratic parties of all countries.

The Communists disdain to conceal their views and aims. They openly declare that their ends can be attained only by the forcible over-throw of all existing social conditions. Let the ruling classes tremble at a communistic revolution. The proletarians have nothing to lose but their chains. They have a world to win.

WORKERS OF ALL COUNTRIES, UNITE!

---

1. By bourgeoisie is meant the class of modern capitalists, owners of the means of social production and employers of wage labor. By proletariat, the class of modern wage laborers who, having no means of production of their own, are reduced to selling their labor power in order to live. (Engels, 1888 English edition)

2. That is, all *written* history. In 1847, the prehistory of society, the social organization existing previous to recorded history, was all but unknown. Since then, [August von] Haxthausen [1792–1866] discovered common ownership of land in Russia, [Georg Ludwig von] Maurer proved it to be the social foundation from which all Teutonic races started in history, and, by and by, village communities were found to be, or to have been,

the primitive form of society everywhere from India to Ireland. The inner organization of this primitive communistic society was laid bare, in its typical form, by [Lewis Henry] Morgan's [1818–61] crowning discovery of the true nature of the *gens* and its relation to the *tribe*. With the dissolution of these primeval communities, society begins to be differentiated into separate and finally antagonistic classes. I have attempted to retrace this dissolution in *The Origin of the Family, Private Property and the State*, Second Edition, Stuttgart, 1886. (Engels, 1888 English edition)

3. Guild-master, that is, a full member of a guild, a master within, not a head of a guild. (Engels, 1888 English edition)

4. "Commune" was the name taken, in France, by the nascent towns even before they had conquered, from their feudal lords and masters, local self-government and political rights as the "third estate." Generally speaking, for the economical development of the bourgeoisie, England is here taken as the typical country; for its political development, France. (Engels, 1888 English edition)

5. Not the English Restoration (1660–89), but the French Restoration (1814–30). (Engels, 1888 German edition)

6. This applies chiefly to Germany, where the landed aristocracy and squirearchy have large portions of their estates cultivated for their own account by stewards, and are, moreover, extensive beet-sugar manufacturers and distillers of potato spirits. The wealthier British aristocracy are, as yet, rath-er above that; but they, too, know how to make up for declining rents by lending their names to floaters of more or less shady joint-stock companies. (Engels, 1888 German edition)

7. The revolutionary storm of 1848 swept away this whole shabby tendency and cured its protagonists of the desire to dabble in socialism. The chief representative and classical type of this tendency is Mr. Karl Grün. (Engels, 1888 German edition)

8. *Phalanstères* were socialist colonies on the plan of Charles Fourier; Icaria was the name given by Cabet to his utopia and, later on, to his American communist colony. (Engels)

9. The party then represented in parliament by Ledru-Rollin, in literature by Louis Blanc, in the daily press by *La Réforme. The name "Social Democracy" signified, with these its inventors, a section of the democratic or republican party more or less tinged with socialism. (Engels, 1888 English edition)*

reform or revolution

ROSA LUXEMBURG

Written as a critique of Eduard Bernstein's revisionism of classical Marxism, this essay first appeared as a series of articles in September 1898 and April 1899. Bernstein (1850–1932) was a leading figure in the German socialist movement who had been named Marx's literary executor by Friedrich Engels. After Engels' death — especially in a series of essays published during 1896–98 under the title of "Problems of Socialism" — Bernstein called for a rejection of many of Marx's concepts in light of a suggested stability of capitalism and the growth of Social Democracy. Bernstein's theory was later published in book form as *Evolutionary Socialism*.

The first book edition of Rosa Luxemburg's *Reform or Revolution* was pub-lished in 1899. A second revised edition — with corrections by Luxemburg — was published in 1908.

INTRODUCTION

AT FIRST VIEW, the title of this work may be surprising. Social reform *or* revolution? Can Social Democracy be *against* reforms? Can it *oppose* social revolution, the transformation of the existing order, its final goal, to social reforms? Certainly not. The daily struggle for reforms, for the amelioration of the condition of the workers within the framework of the existing social order, and for democratic institutions, offers Social Democracy the only means of engaging in the proletarian class war and working in the direction of the final goal — the conquest of political power and the suppression of wage labor. For Social Democracy there exists an indissoluble tie between social reform and revolution. The struggle for reforms is its *means*; the social revolution, its *goal*.

It is in Eduard Bernstein's theory, presented in his articles on "Problems of Socialism," in *Neue Zeit* of 1897–98, and in his book *The Preconditions of Socialism and the Tasks of Social Democracy* that we find, for the first time, the opposition of the two moments of the labor movement. His theory tends to counsel the renunciation of the social transformation, the final goal of Social Democracy, and, inversely, to make social reforms, which are the *means* of the class struggle, into its *end*. Bernstein himself very clearly and characteristically formulated this viewpoint when he wrote: "The final goal, whatever it may be, is nothing to me; the movement is everything."

But since the final goal of socialism is the only decisive factor distinguishing the Social Democratic movement from bourgeois democracy and from bourgeois radicalism, the only factor transforming the entire labor movement from a vain effort to repair the capitalist order into a class struggle *against* this order, for the suppression of this order — the question "Reform or Revolution?" as it is posed by Bernstein, equals for Social Democracy the question "To be or not to be?" In the controversy with Bernstein and his followers, everybody in the Party ought to understand clearly it is not a question of this or that method of struggle, or the use of this or that *tactic*, but of the very *existence* of the Social Democratic movement.

From a casual consideration of Bernstein's theory, this may appear like an exaggeration. Does he not continually mention Social Democracy and its aims? Does he not repeat again and again, in very explicit language, that he too strives toward the final goal of socialism, but in another way? Does he not stress particularly that he fully approves of the present practice of Social Democracy?

That is all true, to be sure. But it is also true that every new movement, when it first elaborates its theory and policy, begins by finding support in the preceding movement, though it may be in direct contradiction with the latter. It begins by suiting itself to the forms already at hand, and by speaking the language previously spoken. In time, the new grain breaks through the old husk. The new movement finds its own forms and its own language.

To expect an opposition against scientific socialism, at its very beginning, to express itself clearly, fully and to the last consequence; to expect it to *deny* openly and bluntly the theoretical basis of Social Democracy — would amount to underrating the power of scientific socialism. Today, those who would pass as a socialist, and at the same time would declare war on Marxian doctrine, the most stupendous product of the human mind in this century, must begin with involuntary esteem for Marxism. They must begin by acknowledging themselves to be its disciple, by seeking in Marx's own teachings the points of support for an attack on them, representing this attack as a further development of Marxian doctrine. On this account, unconcerned by its outer forms, one must pick out the sheathed kernel of Bernstein's theory. This is a matter of urgent necessity for the broad strata of the industrial proletariat in our Party.

No coarser insult, no baser defamation, can be thrown against the workers than the remark, "Theoretical controversies are only for intellectuals." Lassalle once said, "Only when science and the workers, these opposed poles of society, become one, will they crush in their arms of steel all obstacles to culture." The entire strength of the modern labor movement rests on theoretical knowledge.

But this knowledge is doubly important for the workers in the present case, because it is precisely they and their influence in the movement that are in the balance here. It is their skin that is being brought to market. The opportunist current in the Party, whose theory is formulated by Bernstein, is nothing other than an unconscious attempt to assure the predominance of the petty-bourgeois elements that have entered our Party, to change the policy and aims of our Party in their direction. The question of reform or revolution, of the final goal and the movement, is, in another form, the question of the *petty-bourgeois or proletarian character of the labor movement*.

It is, therefore, in the interest of the proletarian mass of the Party to become acquainted, actively and in detail, with the present theoretical controversy with opportunism. As long as theoretical knowledge remains the privilege of a handful of "intellectuals" in the Party, it will face the danger of going astray. Only when the great mass of workers take the keen and dependable weapons of scientific socialism in their own hands, will all the petty-bourgeois inclinations, all the opportunistic currents, come to naught. The movement will then find itself on sure and firm ground. "Quantity will do it."

Berlin, April 18, 1899

PART ONE: THE OPPORTUNIST METHOD

If it is true that theories are reflections in the human consciousness of the phenomena of the exterior world, then it must be added, concerning Eduard Bernstein's theory, that these theories are sometimes inverted images. Think of a theory of instituting socialism by means of social reforms in the face of the complete stagnation of the reform movement in Germany. Think of a theory of trade union control over production in face of the defeat of metal workers in England. Consider the theory of winning a majority in parliament, after the revision of the constitution of Saxony and in view of the most recent attempts against universal suffrage. The pivotal point of Bernstein's system, however, is not located in his conception of the practical tasks of Social Democracy. It is found in his stand on the course of the objective development of capitalist society which, of course, is closely bound to his conception of the practical tasks of Social Democracy.

According to Bernstein, a general breakdown of capitalism seems to be increasingly improbable because, on the one hand, capitalism shows a greater capacity of adaptation, and, on the other hand, capitalist production becomes more and more varied.

The capacity of capitalism to adapt itself, says Bernstein, is manifested first in the disappearance of general crises, thanks to the development of the credit system, employers' organizations, wider means of communication and informational services. It shows itself secondly in the tenacity of the middle classes, which follows from the growing differentiation of the branches of production and the elevation of vast strata of the proletariat into the middle class. It is furthermore proved, argues Bernstein, by the amelioration of the economic and political situation of the proletariat as a result of its trade union activity.

From this theoretical stand is derived the following general conclusion about the practical struggle of Social Democracy. It must not direct its daily activity toward the conquest of political power but toward the improvement of the condition of the working class, within the existing order. It must not expect to institute socialism as a result of a political and social crisis, but should build socialism by means of the progressive extension of social control and the gradual application of the principle of cooperation.

Bernstein himself sees nothing new in his theories. On the contrary, he believes them to be in agreement with certain declarations of Marx and Engels, as well as with the general direction of Social Democracy up to the present. Nevertheless, it seems to us that it is difficult to deny that they are in formal contradiction with the conceptions of scientific socialism.

If Bernstein's revisionism consisted merely in affirming that the march of capitalist development is slower than was thought before, he would merely be presenting an argument for adjourning the conquest of power by the proletariat on which everybody up to now has agreed. Its only consequence would be a slowing of the pace of the struggle.

But that is not the case. What Bernstein questions is not the rapidity of the development of capitalist society, but the path of the development itself and, consequently, the very possibility of a transition to socialism.

Socialist theory up to now declared that the point of departure for a transformation to socialism would be a general and catastrophic crisis. We must distinguish in this outlook two things: the fundamental idea and its exterior form.

The fundamental idea consists of the affirmation that capitalism, as a result of its own inner contradictions, moves toward a point when it will be unbalanced, when it will simply become impossible. There were good reasons for thinking of that juncture in the form of a catastrophic general commercial crisis. But, nonetheless, that is of secondary importance and inessential to the fundamental idea.

As is well known, the scientific basis of socialism rests on *three* results of capitalist development. First, and most important, on the growing *anarchy* of the capitalist economy, leading inevitably to its ruin. Second, on the progressive *socialization* of the process of production, which creates the germs of the future social order. And third, on the growing *organization and class consciousness* of the proletariat, which constitutes the active factor in the coming revolution.

Bernstein eliminates the first of the three fundamental supports of scientific socialism. He says that capitalist development does not lead to a general economic collapse.

He does not merely reject a certain form of the collapse. He rejects the very possibility of collapse. He says, textually: "One could object that by collapse of the present society is meant something else than a general commercial crisis worse than all others, namely, a complete collapse of the capitalist system brought about as a result of its own contradictions." And to this he replies: "With the growing development of society a complete and almost general collapse of the present system of production becomes not more but less probable, because capitalist development increases, on the one hand, the capacity of adaptation and, on the other — that is, at the same time, the differentiation of industry."[1]

But then the important question arises: Why and how shall we attain the final goal of our efforts? According to scientific socialism, the historical necessity of the socialist revolution manifests itself above all in the growing anarchy of capitalism, which drives the system into an impasse. But if one admits, with Bernstein, that capitalist development does not move in the direction of its own ruin, then socialism ceases to be *objectively necessary*. There remain only the other two mainstays of the scientific explanation of socialism, which are also consequences of the capitalism order: the socialization of the process of production and the class consciousness of the proletariat. It is these that Bernstein has in mind when he says that with the elimination of the breakdown theory, "The socialist doctrine loses nothing of its power of persuasion. For, examined closely, what are all the factors enumerated by us that make for the suppression or the modification of the former crises? Nothing else, in fact, than the preconditions, or even in part the germs, of the socialization of production and exchange."[2]

Very little reflection is needed to see that this, too, is a false conclusion. Where does the importance of all the phenomena which Bernstein says are the means of capitalist adaptation — cartels, the credit system, the development of means of communication, the amelioration of the situation of the working class, etc. — lie? Obviously in that they eliminate or, at least, attenuate the internal contradictions of capitalist economy, and stop the development or the aggravation of these contradictions. Thus the elimination of crises means the suppression of the antagonism between production and exchange on the capitalist base. The amelioration of the situation of the working class, or the penetration of certain fractions of the class into middle layers, means the attenuation of the antagonism between capital and labor. But if the cartels, credit system, trade unions, etc., suppress the capitalist contradictions and consequently save the system from ruin; if they enable capitalism to maintain itself — and that is why Bernstein calls them "means of adaptation" — how can they be at the same time "the preconditions, or even in part the germs" of socialism? Obviously only in the sense that they express more clearly the social character of production.

But, inversely, by maintaining it in its capitalist form, the same factors render superfluous in equal measure the transformation of this socialized production into socialist production. That is why they can be the germs or preconditions of a socialist order only in a conceptual sense and not in a historical sense. They are phenomena which, in the light of our conception of socialism, we *know* to be related to socialism but which, in fact, not only do not lead to a socialist revolution but, on the contrary, render it superfluous.

There remains only one foundation of socialism — the class consciousness of the proletariat. But it, too, is in the given case not the simple intellectual reflection of the ever growing contradictions of capitalism and its approaching decline — for this decline is prevented by the means of adaptation. It is now a mere ideal whose force of persuasion rests only on the perfection attributed to it.

We have here, in brief, the explanation of the socialist program by means of "pure reason." We have here, to use simpler language, an idealist explanation of socialism. The objective necessity of socialism, the explanation of socialism as the result of the material development of society, falls away.

Revisionist theory thus places itself in a dilemma. Either the socialist transformation is, as was admitted up to now, the consequence of the internal contradictions of the capitalist order — then with this order will develop its contradictions, resulting inevitably, at some point, in its collapse. In this case, however, the "means of adaptation" are ineffective and the breakdown theory is correct. Or, the "means of adaptation" are really capable of stopping the breakdown of the capitalist system and thereby enable capitalism to maintain itself by suppressing its own contradictions. In that case, *socialism* ceases to be a historical necessity. It then becomes anything you want to call it, except the result of the material development of society.

The dilemma leads to another. Either revisionism is correct concerning the course of capitalist development, and therefore the socialist transformation of society is only a utopia. Or, socialism is not a utopia, and therefore the theory of "means of adaptation" is false. "That is the question."

The Adaptation of Capitalism

According to Bernstein, the credit system, the improved means of communication and the new employers' organizations are the important factors that bring about the adaptation of the capitalist economy.

Credit has diverse functions in the capitalist economy. Its two most important functions, as is well known, are to increase the capacity to expand production and to facilitate exchange. When the inner tendency of capitalist production to expand limitlessly strikes against the barrier of private property (the limited dimensions of private capital), credit appears as a means of surmounting these limits in a particular capitalist manner. Credit, through shareholding, combines in one mass of capital a large number of individual capitals. It makes available to each capitalist the use of other capitalists' money — in the form of industrial credit. Further, as commercial credit, it accelerates the exchange of commodities and therefore the return of capital into production, and thus aids the entire cycle of the process of production.

The manner in which these two principal functions of credit influence the formation of crises is quite obvious. If it is true that crises appear as a result of the contradiction between the capacity for expansion, the tendency of production to increase, and the restricted consumption capacity of the market, then in view of what was stated above, credit is precisely the specific means of making this contradiction break out as often as possible. To begin with, it increases the capacity for the expansion of production disproportionately and thus constitutes an inner driving force that constantly pushes production to exceed the limits of the market. But credit strikes from two sides. After having (as a factor of the process of production) provoked overproduction, credit (as a factor of exchange) destroys, during the crisis, the very productive forces it itself created. At the first symptom of the crisis, credit melts away. It abandons the exchange process just when it is still indispensable, and where it still exists, it shows itself instead ineffective and useless, and thus during the crisis it reduces to a minimum the consumption capacity of the market.

Besides these two principal results, credit also influences the formation of crises in the following ways. It constitutes the technical means of making available to an entrepreneur the capital of other owners. It stimulates at the same time the bold and unscrupulous utilization of the property of others. That is, it leads to reckless speculation. Credit not only aggravates the crisis in its capacity as a dissembled means of exchange, it also helps to bring on and extend the crisis by transforming all exchange into an extremely complex and artificial mechanism that, having a minimum of metallic money as a real base, is easily disarranged at the slightest occasion.

Thus, far from being an instrument for the elimination or the attenuation of crises, credit is on the contrary a particularly powerful factor in the formation of crises. This could not possibly be otherwise. Credit eliminates the remaining rigidity of capitalist relationships. It introduces everywhere the greatest elasticity possible. It renders all capitalist forces extendable, relative and sensitive to the highest degree. Doing this, it facilitates and aggravates crises, which are nothing but the periodic collisions of the contradictory forces of capitalist economy.

This leads, at the same time, to another question. How can credit generally have the appearance of a "means of adaptation" of capitalism? No matter in what context or form this "adaptation" is conceived, its essence can obviously only be that one of the several antagonistic relations of capitalist economy is smoothed over, that one of its contradictions is suppressed or weakened, and that thus liberty of movement is assured, at one point or another, to the otherwise fettered productive forces. In fact, it is precisely credit that aggravates these contradictions to the highest degree. It aggravates the antagonism between the *mode of production* and the *mode of exchange* by stretching production to the limit and at the same time paralyzing exchange on the smallest pretext. It increases the contradiction between the *mode of production* and the *mode of appropriation* by separating production from ownership, that is, by transforming the capital employed in production into "social" capital and at the same time transforming a part of the profit, in the form of interest on capital, into a simple title of ownership. It increases the contradiction between the *property relations* and the *relations of production* by putting immense productive forces into a small number of hands and expropriating large numbers of small capitalists. It increases the contradiction between the social character of production and capitalist *private ownership* by rendering necessary the intervention of the state in production (stock companies).

In short, credit reproduces all the fundamental antagonisms of the capitalist world. It accentuates them. It precipitates their development and thus pushes the capitalist world forward to its own destruction —

the breakdown. The prime act of capitalist adaptation, as far as credit is concerned, should really consist in breaking and *suppressing* credit. In fact, credit is far from being a means of capitalist adaptation. As it presently exists it is, on the contrary, a means of destruction of the most extreme revolutionary significance. Has not precisely this revolutionary character which leads the credit system beyond capitalism actually inspired plans of "socialist" reform? As such, it has had some distinguished proponents, some of whom (Isaac Pereire in France), were, as Marx put it, half prophets, half rogues.

Just as fragile is the second "means of adaptation": employers' organizations. According to Bernstein, such organizations will put an end to anarchy of production and do away with crises through the regulation of production. It is true that the multiple repercussions of the development of cartels and trusts have not been studied too carefully up to now. But they represent a problem that can only be solved with the aid of Marxist theory.

One thing is certain. We could speak of a damming up of capitalist anarchy by employers' organizations only in the measure that cartels, trusts, etc., become, even approximately, the dominant form of production. But such a possibility is excluded by the very nature of the cartels. The final economic aim and result of employers' organizations is the following. Through the elimination of competition in a given branch of production, the distribution of the mass of profit realized on the market is influenced in such a manner that there is an increase of the share going to this branch of industry. Such organization can only increase the rate of profit in one branch of industry at the expense of another. That is precisely why it cannot be generalized, for when it is extended to all important branches of industry, this tendency cancels its own influence.

But even within the limits of their practical application, the result of employers' organizations is the very opposite of the elimination of industrial anarchy. Cartels ordinarily succeed in obtaining an increase of the rate of profit in the internal market by producing at a lower rate

of profit for the foreign market, thus utilizing the supplementary portions of capital which they cannot utilize for domestic needs. That is to
say, they sell abroad cheaper than at home. The result is the sharpening
of competition abroad and an increased anarchy on the world market
— the very opposite of what is intended. This is well demonstrated by
the history of the international sugar industry.

Generally speaking, employers' organizations, as a manifestation
of the capitalist mode of production, can only be considered a definite
phase of capitalist development. Cartels are fundamentally nothing
but a means resorted to by the capitalist mode of production to hold
back the fatal fall of the rate of profit in certain branches of production.
What method do cartels employ to this end? That of keeping inactive
a part of the accumulated capital. That is, they use the same method
which, in another form, comes into play during crises. The remedy and
the illness resemble each other like two drops of water. Indeed the first
can be considered the lesser evil only up to a certain point. When the
market outlets begin to shrink, and the world market has been extended
to its limit and has been exhausted by the competition of the capitalist
countries — and sooner or later this is bound to occur — then the forced
partial idleness of capital will reach such dimensions that the remedy
will become transformed into an illness, and capital, already pretty
much "socialized" through regulation, will tend to revert again to the
form of private capital. In the face of the increased difficulties of finding
markets, each individual portion of capital will prefer to take its chances
alone. At that time, the [employers'] organizations will burst like soap
bubbles and give way to free competition in an aggravated form.

In a general way, cartels, just like credit, appear therefore as a
determined phase of capitalist development, which in the last analysis aggravates the anarchy of the capitalist world and expresses and
ripens its internal contradictions. Cartels aggravate the contradiction
between the mode of production and exchange by sharpening the
struggle between the producer and consumer, as is the case especially
in the United States. They aggravate, furthermore, the contradiction

between the mode of production and the mode of appropriation by opposing the superior force of organized capital to the working class in the most brutal fashion, and thus increasing the antagonism between capital and labor.

Finally, capitalist cartels aggravate the contradiction between the international character of the capitalist world economy and the national character of the capitalist state — insofar as they are always accompanied by a general tariff war, which sharpens the differences among the capitalist states. We must add to this the decidedly revolutionary influence exercised by cartels on the concentration of production, technical progress, etc.

In other words, when evaluated from the angle of their final effect on capitalist economy, cartels and trusts fail as "means of adaptation." They fail to attenuate the contradictions of capitalism. On the contrary, they appear to be an instrument of greater anarchy. They encourage the further development of the internal contradictions of capitalism and accelerate the coming of a general decline of capitalism.

But if the credit system, cartels and the rest do not suppress the anarchy of capitalism, why have we not had a major commercial crisis for two decades, since 1873? Is this not a sign that, contrary to Marx's analysis, the capitalist mode of production has adapted itself — at least in a general way — to the needs of society? Hardly had Bernstein rejected, in 1898, Marx's theory of crises, when a profound general crisis broke out in 1900, while seven years later, a new crisis beginning in the United States hit the world market. Facts proved the theory of "adaptation" to be false. At the same time they showed that the people who abandoned Marx's theory of crisis only because no crisis occurred within a certain space of time merely confused the essence of this theory with one of its secondary exterior aspects — the 10-year cycle. The description of the cycle of modern capitalist industry as a 10-year period was to Marx and Engels, in 1860 and 1870, only a simple statement of facts. It was not based on a natural law but on a series of given historical circumstances that were connected with the rapidly spreading activity of young capitalism.

The crisis of 1825 was, in effect, the result of extensive investment of capital in the construction of roads, canals, gasworks, which took place during the preceding decade, particularly in England, where the crisis broke out. The following crisis of 1836–39 was similarly the result of heavy investments in the construction of means of transportation. The crisis of 1847 was provoked by the feverish building of railroads in England (from 1844 to 1847, in three years, the British Parliament gave railway concessions to the value of 15 billion dollars). In each of the three mentioned cases, a crisis came after new bases for capitalist development were established. In 1857, the same result was brought by the abrupt opening of new markets for European industry in America and Australia, after the discovery of the gold mines, and the extensive construction of railway lines, especially in France, where the example of England was then closely imitated. (From 1852 to 1856, new railway lines to the value of 1,250 million francs were built in France alone.) And finally we have the great crisis of 1873 — a direct consequence of the firm boom of large industry in Germany and Austria, which followed the political events of 1866 and 1871.

So that up to now, the sudden extension of the domain of capitalist economy, and not its shrinking, was each time the cause of the commercial crisis. That the international crises repeated themselves precisely every 10 years was a purely exterior fact, a matter of chance. The Marxist formula for crises as presented by Engels in *Anti-Dühring* and by Marx in the first and third volumes of *Capital*, applies to all crises only in the measure that it uncovers their international mechanism and their general basic causes.

Crises may repeat themselves every five or 10 years, or even every eight or 20 years. But what proves best the falseness of Bernstein's theory is that it is in the countries having the greatest development of the famous "means of adaptation" — credit, perfected communications and trusts — that the last crisis (1907–08) was most violent.

The belief that capitalist production could "adapt" itself to exchange presupposes one of two things: either the world market can spread unlimitedly, or on the contrary the development of the productive forces is so fettered that it cannot pass beyond the bounds of the market. The first hypothesis constitutes a material impossibility. The second is rendered just as impossible by the constant technical progress that daily creates new productive forces in all branches.

There remains still another phenomenon which, says Bernstein, contradicts the course of capitalist development as it is indicated above. In the "steadfast phalanx" of middle-size enterprises, Bernstein sees a sign that the development of large industry does not move in a revolutionary direction, and is not as effective from the angle of the concentration of industry as was expected by the " break-down theory." He is here, however, the victim of his own lack of understanding. For to see the progressive disappearance of the middle–size enterprise as a necessary result of the development of large industry is to misunderstand sadly the nature of this process.

According to Marxist theory, small capitalists play the role of pioneers of technical revolution in the general course of capitalist development. They play that role in a double sense. They initiate new methods of production in well-established branches of industry; they are instrumental in the creation of new branches of production not yet exploited by the big capitalist. It is false to imagine that the history of the middle-size capitalist establishments proceeds unequivocally in the direction of their progressive disappearance. The course of their development is on the contrary purely dialectical and moves constantly among contradictions. The middle capitalist layers, just like the workers, find themselves under the influence of two antagonistic tendencies, one ascendant and the other descendant. In this case, the descendent tendency is the continued rise in the scale of production which periodically overflows the dimensions of the average-size capital and removes it repeatedly from the competitive terrain.

The ascendant tendency is, first, the periodic depreciation of the existing capital which again lowers, for a certain time, the scale of production in proportion to the value of the necessary minimum amount of capital. It is also represented by the penetration of capitalist production into new spheres. The struggle of the average-size enterprise against big capital cannot be considered a regularly proceeding battle in which the troops of the weaker party continue to melt away directly and quantitatively. It should rather be regarded as a periodic mowing down of the small enterprises, which rapidly grow up again, only to be mowed down once more by large industry. The two tendencies play ball with the middle capitalist layers. The descending tendency must win in the end.

The very opposite is true about the development of the working class. The victory of the descending tendency need not necessarily show itself in an absolute numerical diminution of the middle-size enterprises. It must show itself, first, in the progressive increase of the minimum amount of capital necessary for the functioning of the enterprises in the old branches of production; second, in the constant diminution of the interval of time during which the small capitalists conserve the opportunity to exploit the new branches of production. The result, as far as the small capitalist is concerned, is a progressively shorter duration of his economic life and an ever more rapid change in the methods of production and of investment. For the average capitalist strata, taken as a whole, there is a process of more and more rapid social metabolism.

Bernstein knows this perfectly well. He himself comments on this. But what he seems to forget is that this very thing is the law of the movement of the average capitalist enterprise. If small capitalists are the pioneers of technical progress, and if technical progress is the vital pulse of the capitalist economy, then it is manifest that small capitalists are an integral part of capitalist development. The progressive disappearance of the middle-size enterprise — in the absolute sense considered by Bernstein — would not mean, as he thinks, the revolutionary advance of capitalist development, but precisely the contrary, the cessation, the slowing down of development. "The rate of profit, that is to say, the relative increase of capital," said Marx, "is important first of all for new investors of capital grouping themselves independently. And as soon as the formation of capital falls exclusively into a handful of big capitalists, the revivifying fire of production is extinguished. It dies away."

The Realization of Socialism Through Social Reforms

Bernstein rejects the "breakdown theory" as a historical road toward socialism. Now what is the way to a socialist society that is proposed by his "theory of adaptation to capitalism"? Bernstein answers this question only by allusion. Konrad Schmidt, however, attempts to deal with this detail in the manner of Bernstein. According to him, "the trade union struggle for hours and wages and the political struggle for reforms will lead to a progressively more extensive control over the conditions of production," and "as the rights of the capitalist proprietor will be diminished through legislation, he will be reduced in time to the role of a simple administrator." "The capitalist will see his property lose more and more value to himself" till finally "the direction and administration of exploitation will be taken from him entirely" and "collective exploitation" instituted.

Therefore trade unions, social reforms and, adds Bernstein, the political democratization of the state are the means of the progressive realization of socialism.

But the fact is that the principal function of trade unions (and this was best explained by Bernstein himself in *Neue Zeit* in 1891) consists in providing the workers with a means of realizing the capitalist law of wages, that is to say, the sale of their labor power at current market prices. Trade unions enable the proletariat to utilize at each instant the conjuncture of the market. But these conjunctures — 1) the labor demand determined by the state of production, 2) the labor supply created by the proletarianization of the middle strata of society and the natural reproduction of the working classes, and 3) the momentary degree of productivity of labor — these remain outside of the sphere of influence of the trade unions. Trade unions cannot suppress the law of wages. Under the most favorable circumstances, the best they can do is to impose on capitalist exploitation the "normal" limit of the moment. They do not have, however, the power to suppress exploitation itself, not even gradually.

Schmidt, it is true, sees the present trade union movement in a "feeble initial stage." He hopes that "in the future" the "trade union movement will exercise a progressively increased influence over the regulation of production." But by the regulation of production we can only understand two things: intervention in the technical domain of the process of production and fixing the scale of production itself. What is the nature of the influence exercised by trade unions in these two departments? It is clear that in the technique of production, the inter- est of the capitalist agrees, up to a certain point, with the progress and development of capitalist economy. It is his own interest that pushes him to make technical improvements. But the isolated worker finds himself in a decidedly different position. Each technical transforma- tion contradicts his interests. It aggravates his helpless situation by depreciating the value of his labor power and rendering his work more intense, more monotonous and more difficult.

Insofar as trade unions can intervene in the technical department of production, they can only oppose technical innovation. But here they do not act in the interest of the entire working class and its emancipation, which accords rather with technical progress and, therefore, with the interest of the isolated capitalist. They act here in a reactionary direc- tion. And, in fact, we find efforts on the part of workers to intervene in the technical part of production not in the future, where Schmidt looks for it, but in the past of the trade union movement. Such efforts characterized the old phase of English trade unionism (up to 1860), when the British organizations were still tied to medieval "corpora- tive" vestiges and found inspiration in the outworn principle of "a fair day's wage for a fair day's labor," as expressed by Webb in his *History of Trade Unionism.*

On the other hand, the effort of the labor unions to fix the scale of production and the prices of commodities is a recent phenomenon. Only recently have we witnessed such attempts — and again in England. In their nature and tendencies, these efforts resemble those dealt with above. What does the active participation of trade unions in fixing the scale and cost of production amount to? It amounts to a cartel of the workers and entrepreneurs in a common stand against the consumer and especially rival entrepreneurs. In no way is the effect of this any different from that of ordinary employers' organizations. Basically we no longer have here a struggle between labor and capital, but the solidarity of capital and labor against the total consumers. Considered for its social worth, it is seen to be a reactionary move that cannot be a stage in the struggle for the emancipation of the proletariat, because it connotes the very opposite of the class struggle. Considered from the angle of practical application, it is found to be a utopia which, as shown by a rapid examination, cannot be extended to the large branches of industry producing for the world market.

So that the scope of trade unions is limited essentially to a struggle for an increase of wages and the reduction of labor time, that is to say, to efforts at regulating capitalist exploitation as they are made necessary by the momentary situation of the old world market. But labor unions can in no way influence the process of production itself. Moreover, trade union development moves — contrary to what is asserted by Konrad Schmidt — in the direction of a complete detachment of the labor market from any immediate relation to the rest of the market.

That is shown by the fact that even attempts to relate labor contracts to the general situation of production by means of a system of sliding wage scales have been outmoded with historical development. The British labor unions are moving farther and farther away from such efforts.

Even within the effective boundaries of its activity the trade union movement cannot spread in the unlimited way claimed for it by the theory of adaptation. On the contrary, if we examine the large factors of social development, we see that we are not moving toward an epoch marked by a victorious development of trade unions, but rather toward a time when the hardships of labor unions will increase. Once industrial development has attained its highest possible point and capitalism has entered its descending phase on the world market, the trade union struggle will become doubly difficult. In the first place, the objective conjuncture of the market will be less favorable to the sellers of labor power, because the demand for labor power will increase at a slower rate and labor supply more rapidly than at present. In the second place, the capitalists themselves, in order to make up for losses suffered on the world market, will make even greater efforts than at present to reduce the part of the total product going to the workers (in the form of wages). The reduction of wages is, as pointed out by Marx, one of the principal means of retarding the fall of profit. The situation in England already offers us a picture of the beginning of the second stage of trade union development. Trade union action is reduced of necessity to the simple defense of already realized gains, and even that is becoming more and more difficult. Such is the general trend of things in our society. The counterpart of this tendency should be the development of the political side of the class struggle.

Konrad Schmidt commits the same error of historical perspective when he deals with social reforms. He expects that social reforms, like trade union organizations, will "dictate to the capitalists the only conditions under which they will be able to employ labor power." Seeing reform in this light, Bernstein calls labor legislation a piece of "social control," and as such, a piece of socialism. Similarly, Konrad Schmidt always uses the term "social control" when he refers to labor protection laws. Once he has thus happily transformed the state into society, he confidently adds: "That is to say, the rising working class." As a result of this trick of substitution, the innocent labor laws enacted by the German Federal Council are transformed into transitory socialist measures supposedly enacted by the German proletariat.

The mystification is obvious. We know that the present state is not "society" representing the "rising working class." It is itself the representative of capitalist society. It is a class state. Therefore its reform measures are not an application of "social control," that is, the control of society working freely in its own labor process. They are forms of control applied by the class organization of capital to the production of capital. The so-called social reforms are enacted in the interests of capital. Yes, Bernstein and Konrad Schmidt see at present only "feeble beginnings" of this control. They hope to see a long succession of reforms in the future, all favoring the working class. But here they commit a mistake similar to their belief in the unlimited development of the trade union movement.

A basic condition for the theory of the gradual realization of socialism through social reforms is a certain objective development of capitalist property and of the state. Konrad Schmidt says that the capitalist proprietor tends to lose his special rights with historical development, and is reduced to the role of a simple administrator. He thinks that the expropriation of the means of production cannot possibly be effected as a single historical act. He therefore resorts to the theory of expropriation by stages. With this in mind, he divides the right to property into 1) the right of "sovereignty" (ownership) — which he attributes to a thing called "society" and which he wants to extend, and 2) its opposite, the simple right of *use*, held by the capitalist, but which is supposedly being reduced in the hands of the capitalists to the mere administration of their enterprises.

This interpretation is either a simple play on words, and in that case the theory of gradual expropriation has no real basis, or it is a true picture of juridical development, in which case, as we shall see, the theory of gradual expropriation is entirely false.

The division of the right of property into several component rights, an arrangement serving Konrad Schmidt as a shelter wherein he may construct his theory of "expropriation by stages," characterized feudal society, founded on natural economy. In feudalism, the total product was shared among the social classes of the time on the basis of the personal relations existing between the feudal lord and his serfs or tenants. The decomposition of property into several partial rights reflected the manner of distribution of the social wealth of that period. With the passage to the production of commodities and the dissolution of all personal bonds among the participants in the process of production, the relation between men and things (that is to say, private property) became reciprocally stronger. Since the division is no longer made on the basis of personal relations but through exchange, the different rights to a share in the social wealth are no longer measured as fragments of property rights having a common interest. They are measured now according to the values brought by each on the market.

The first change introduced into juridical relations with the advance of commodity production in the medieval city communes, was the development of absolute private property. The latter appeared in the very midst of the feudal juridical relations. This development has progressed at a rapid pace in capitalist production. The more the process of production is socialized, the more the process of distribution (division of wealth) rests on exchange. And the more private property becomes inviolable and closed, the more capitalist property becomes transformed from the right to the product of one's own labor to the simple right to appropriate somebody else's labor. As long as the capitalist himself manages his own factory, distribution is still, up to a certain point, tied to his personal participation in the process of production. But as the personal management on the part of the capitalist becomes superfluous — which is the case in the shareholding societies today — the property of capital, so far as its right to share in the distribution (division of wealth) is concerned, becomes separated from any personal relation with production. It now appears in its purest form. The capitalist right to property reaches its most complete development in capital held in the shape of shares and industrial credit.

Konrad Schmidt's historical schema, tracing the transformation of the capitalist "from a proprietor to a simple administrator," belies the real historical development. In historical reality, on the contrary, the capitalist tends to change from a proprietor and administrator to a simple proprietor. What happens here to Konrad Schmidt, happened to Goethe:

> What is, he sees as in a dream.
> What no longer is, becomes for him reality.

Just as Schmidt's historical schema travels, economically, backwards from a modern shareholding society to an artisan's shop, so, juridically, he wishes to lead back the capitalist world into the old feudal shell of the Middle Ages.

Also from this point of view, "social control" appears in reality under a different aspect than seen by Konrad Schmidt. What functions today as "social control" — labor legislation, the control of industrial organizations through share holding, etc. — has absolutely nothing to do with his "supreme ownership." Far from being, as Schmidt believes, a reduction of capitalist ownership, his "social control" is, on the contrary, a protection of such ownership. Or, expressed from the economic viewpoint, it is not a threat to capitalist exploitation, but simply the regulation of this exploitation. When Bernstein asks if there is more or less of socialism in a labor protective law, we can assure him that, in the best of labor protective laws, there is no more "socialism" than in a municipal ordinance regulating the cleaning of streets or the lighting of street lamps.

Capitalism and the State

The second condition of the gradual realization of socialism is, according to Bernstein, the evolution of the state in society. It has become a commonplace to say that the present state is a class state. This, too, like referring to capitalist society, should not be understood in a rigorous absolute manner, but dialectically.

The state became capitalist with the political victory of the bour-geoisie. Capitalist development modifies essentially the nature of the state, widening its sphere of action, constantly imposing on it new functions (especially those affecting economic life), making more and more necessary its intervention and control in society. In this sense, capitalist development prepares little by little the future fusion of the state to society. It prepares, so to say, the return of the function of the state to society. Following this line of thought, one can speak of an evolution of the capitalist state *into* society, and it is undoubtedly what Marx had in mind when he referred to labor legislation as the first conscious intervention of "society" in the vital social process, a phrase upon which Bernstein leans heavily.

On the other hand, the same capitalist development realizes another transformation in the nature of the state. The present state is, first of all, an organization of the ruling class. It assumes functions favoring social development specifically because, and in the measure that, these interests and social developments coincide, in a general fashion, with the interests of the dominant class. Labor legislation is enacted as much in the immediate interest of the capitalist class as in the interest of society in general. But this harmony endures only up to a certain point of capitalist development. When capitalist development has reached a certain level, the interests of the bourgeoisie, as a class, and the needs of economic progress begin to clash even in the capitalist sense. We believe that this phase has already begun. It shows itself in two extremely important phenomena of contemporary social life: on the one hand, the policy of tariff barriers, and on the other, militarism. These two phenomena have played an indispensable, and in that sense a progressive and revolu-tionary role in the history of capitalism. Without tariff protection the development of large industry would have been impossible in several countries. But now the situation is different.

At present, protection does not serve so much to develop young industry as to maintain artificially certain aged forms of production.

From the angle of capitalist development, that is, from the point of view of world economy, it matters little whether Germany exports more merchandise into England or England exports more merchandise into Germany. From the viewpoint of this development it may be said that the blackamoor has done his work and it is time for him to go his way. Given the condition of reciprocal dependence in which the various branches of industry find themselves, a protectionist tariff on any commodity necessarily results in raising the cost of production of other commodities inside the country. It therefore impedes industrial development. But this is not so from the viewpoint of the interests of the capitalist class. While industry does not need tariff barriers for its development, the entrepreneurs need tariffs to protect their markets. This signifies that at present tariffs no longer serve as a means of protecting a developing capitalist section against a more advanced section. They are now the arm used by one national group of capitalists against another group. Furthermore, tariffs are no longer necessary as an instrument of protection for industry in its movement to create and conquer the home market. They are now indispensable means for the cartelization of industry, that is, means used in the struggle of capitalist producers against consuming society in the aggregate. What brings out in an emphatic manner the specific character of contemporary customs policies is the fact that today not industry, but agriculture, plays the predominant role in the making of tariffs. The policy of customs protection has become a tool for converting and expressing the feudal interests in capitalist form.

The same change has taken place in militarism. If we consider history as it was — not as it could have been or should have been — we must agree that war has been an indispensable feature of capitalist development. The United States, Germany, Italy, the Balkan States, Poland, all owe the condition or the rise of their capitalist development to wars, whether resulting in victory or defeat. As long as there were countries marked by internal political division or economic isolation which had to be destroyed, militarism played a revolutionary role, considered from the viewpoint of capitalism. But at present the situation is different. If world politics have become the stage of menacing conflicts, it is not so much a question of the opening of new countries to capitalism. It is a question of already existing *European* antagonisms, which, transported into other lands, have exploded there. The armed opponents we see today in Europe and on other continents do not range themselves as capitalist countries on one side and backward countries on the other. They are states pushed to war especially as a result of their similarly advanced capitalist development. In view of this, an explosion is certain to be fatal to this development, in the sense that it must provoke an extremely profound disturbance and transformation of economic life in all countries.

However, the matter appears entirely different when considered from the standpoint of the *capitalist class*. For the latter militarism has become indispensable. First, as a means of struggle for the defense of "national" interests in competition against other "national" groups. Second, as a method of placement for financial and industrial capital. Third, as an instrument of class domination over the laboring population inside the country. In themselves, these interests have nothing in common with the development of the capitalist mode of production. What demonstrates best the specific character of present day militarism is the fact that it develops generally in all countries as an effect, so to speak, of its own internal, mechanical, motive power, a phenomenon that was completely unknown several decades ago. We recognize this in the fatal character of the impending explosion which is inevitable in spite of the complete indecisiveness of the objectives and motives of the conflict. From a motor of capitalist development militarism has changed into a capitalist illness.

In the clash between capitalist development and the interests of the dominant class, the state takes a position alongside the latter. Its policy, like that of the bourgeoisie, comes into conflict with social development. It thus loses more and more of its character as a representative of the whole of society and is transformed, at the same rate into a pure *class* state. Or, to speak more exactly, these two qualities distinguish themselves more from each other and find themselves in a contradictory relation in the very nature of the state. This contradiction becomes progressively sharper. For on one hand, we have the growth of the functions of a general interest on the part of the state, its intervention in social life, its "control" over society. But on the other hand, its class character obliges the state to move the pivot of its activity and its means of coercion more and more into domains which are useful only to the class character of the bourgeoisie and have for society as a whole only a negative importance, as in the case of militarism and tariff and colonial policies. Moreover, the "social control" exercised by this state is at the same time penetrated with and dominated by its class character (see how labor legislation is applied in all countries).

The extension of democracy, which Bernstein sees as a means of realizing socialism by degrees, does not contradict but, on the contrary, corresponds perfectly to the transformation realized in the nature of the state.

Konrad Schmidt declares that the conquest of a Social Democratic majority in parliament leads directly to the gradual "socialization" of society. Now, the democratic forms of political life are without question a phenomenon expressing clearly the evolution of the state in society. They constitute, to that extent, a move toward a socialist transformation. But the conflict within the capitalist state, described above, manifests itself even more emphatically in modern parliamentarism. Indeed, in accordance with its form, parliamentarism serves to express, within the organization of the state, the interests of the whole society. But what parliamentarism expresses here is capitalist society, that is to say, a society in which capitalist interests predominate. In this society, the representative institutions, democratic in form, are in content the instruments of the interests of the ruling class. This manifests itself in a tangible fashion in the fact that as soon as democracy shows the tendency to negate its class character and become transformed into an instrument of the real interests of the population, the democratic forms are sacrificed by the bourgeoisie, and by its state representatives. That is why the idea of the conquest of a parliamentary reformist majority is a calculation which, entirely in the spirit of bourgeois liberalism, preoccupies itself only with one side — the formal side — of democracy, but does not take into account the other side, its real content. All in all, parliamentarism is not a directly socialist element impregnating gradually the whole capitalist society. It is, on the contrary, a specific form of the bourgeois class state, helping to ripen and develop the existing antagonisms of capitalism.

In the light of the history of the objective development of the state, Bernstein's and Konrad Schmidt's belief that increased "social control" results in the direct introduction of socialism is transformed into a formula that finds itself from day to day in greater contradiction with reality.

The theory of the gradual introduction of socialism proposes progressive reform of capitalist property and the capitalist state in the direction of socialism. But in consequence of the objective laws of existing society, one and the other develop in a precisely opposite direction. The process of production is increasingly socialized, and state intervention, the control of the state over the process of production, is extended. But at the same time, private property becomes more and more the form of open capitalist exploitation of the labor of others, and state control is penetrated with the exclusive interests of the ruling class. The state, that is to say the *political* organization of capitalism, and property relations, that is to say the *juridical* organization of capitalism, become more *capitalist* and not more socialist, two insurmountable difficulties for the theory of the progressive introduction of socialism.

Fourier's scheme of changing, by means of a system of phalansteries, the water of all the seas into tasty lemonade was surely a fantastic idea. But Bernstein, proposing to change the sea of capitalist bitterness into a sea of socialist sweetness, by progressively pouring into it bottles of social reformist lemonade, presents an idea that is merely more insipid but no less fantastic.

The production relations of capitalist society approach more and more the production relations of socialist society. But on the other hand, the political and juridical relations established between capitalist society and socialist society constitute a steadily rising wall. This wall is not overthrown, but is on the contrary strengthened and consolidated by the development of social reforms and the course of democracy. Only the hammer blow of revolution, that is to say, *the conquest of political power by the proletariat,* can break down this wall.

Practical Consequences and General Character of Revisionism

In the first chapter we attempted to show that Bernstein's theory lifts the program of the socialist movement off its material base and places it on an idealist base. This concerns its theoretical foundation. How does this theory appear when translated into practice?

First, and formally, it does not differ in the least from the practice followed by Social Democracy up to now. Trade unions, the struggle for social reform and for the democratization of the political institutions are precisely that which constitutes the formal content of the activity of the Social Democratic Party. The difference is not in the *what,* but in the *how.*

At present, the trade union and the parliamentary struggles are considered to be the means of guiding and educating the proletariat in preparation for the task of taking power. From the revisionist standpoint, this conquest of power is impossible and useless. Therefore, trade union and parliamentary activity are to be carried on only for their immediate results, that is, the bettering of the material situation of the workers, the gradual reduction of capitalist exploitation and the extension of social control.

If we ignore the immediate amelioration of the workers' condition — an objective common to our Party program as well as to revisionism

— the difference between the two conceptions is, in brief, the following. According to the present conception, the socialist significance of trade union and parliamentary activity is that it prepares the proletariat — that is, the *subjective* factor of the socialist transformation — for the task of realizing socialism. According to Bernstein, trade union and political struggles gradually reduce capitalist exploitation itself. They remove from capitalist society its capitalist character, and give it a socialist one. In a word, the two forms of struggle are said to realize the socialist transformation *in an objective sense*.

Examined more closely, the two conceptions are diametrically opposed. In the current conception of our Party, the proletariat becomes convinced of the impossibility of accomplishing fundamental social change as a result of its trade union and parliamentary activity, and arrives at the conviction that these struggles cannot basically change its situation, and that the conquest of power is unavoidable. Bernstein's theory, however, begins by presupposing that this conquest is impossible. It concludes by affirming that the socialist order can only be introduced as a result of the trade union struggle and parliamentary activity. As seen by Bernstein, trade union and parliamentary action has a socialist character because it exercises a progressively socializing influence on the capitalist economy.

We tried to show that this influence is purely imaginary. The structures of capitalist property and the capitalist state develop in entirely opposite directions, so that the daily practical activity of the present Social Democracy loses, in the last analysis, all connection with socialism. The great socialist significance of the trade union and parliamentary struggles is that through them the *awareness*, the consciousness, of the proletariat becomes socialist, and it is organized as a class. But if they are considered as instruments for the direct socialization of capitalist economy, they lose not only their supposed effectiveness but also cease to be a means of preparing the working class for the proletarian conquest of power.

Eduard Bernstein and Konrad Schmidt suffer from a complete misunderstanding when they console themselves with the belief that even though the program of the Party is reduced to work for social reforms and ordinary trade union work, the final objective of the labor movement is not therefore lost, because each forward step reaches beyond the given immediate aim and the socialist goal is implied as a tendency in the movement.

This is certainly true of the present tactic of German Social Democracy in which a firm and conscious effort toward the conquest of political power precedes the trade union struggle and the work for social reforms. But if this presupposed effort is separated from the movement, and social reforms are made an end in themselves, such activity not only does not lead to the realization of socialism as the ultimate goal but moves in a precisely opposite direction.

Konrad Schmidt simply falls back on the idea that an apparently mechanical movement, once started, cannot stop by itself, because "one's appetite grows with the eating," and the working class will supposedly not content itself with reforms till the final socialist transformation is realized.

Now the last mentioned condition is quite real. Its effectiveness is guaranteed by the very insufficiency of capitalist reforms. But the conclusion drawn from it could only be true if it were possible to construct an unbroken chain of augmented reforms leading from the capitalism of today to socialism. This is, of course, sheer fantasy. In accordance with the nature of things, the chain breaks quickly, and the paths that the supposed forward movement can take from that point on are many and varied.

What will be the immediate result should our Party change its general procedure to suit a viewpoint that wants to emphasize the practical results of our struggle, that is social reforms? As soon as "immediate results" become the principal aim of our activity, the clear-cut, irreconcilable class standpoint, which has meaning only insofar as it proposes to win power, will be found more and more an obstacle. The direct consequence of this will be the adoption by the Party of a "policy of compensation," a policy of horse-trading, and an attitude of sage diplomatic conciliation. But the movement cannot remain immobile for long. Since social reforms in the capitalist world are and remain an empty promise, no matter what tactics one uses, the next logical step is necessarily disillusionment in social reform.

It is not true that socialism will arise automatically and under all circumstances from the daily struggle of the working class. Socialism will be the consequence only of the ever growing contradictions of capitalist economy and the comprehension by the working class of the unavoidability of the suppression of these contradictions through a social transformation. When the first condition is denied and the second rejected, as is the case with revisionism, the labor movement is reduced to a simple cooperative and reformist movement, and moves here in a straight line toward the total abandonment of the class standpoint.

These consequences also become clear when we regard revisionism from another side, and ask what is the general character of revisionism. It is obvious that revisionism does not defend capitalist relations. It does not join the bourgeois economists in denying the existence of the contradictions of capitalism. Rather, its theory is based on the presupposition of the existence of these contradictions, just like the Marxist conception. But, on the other hand, what constitutes precisely the fundamental point of revisionism and distinguishes it from the attitude taken by Social Democracy up to now is that it does not base its theory on the suppression of these contradictions as a result of their logical internal development.

We may say that the theory of revisionism occupies an intermediate place between two extremes. Revisionism does not want to see the contradictions of capitalism mature, to *suppress* these contradictions through a revolutionary transformation. It wants to lessen, to *attenuate*, the capitalist contradictions. Thus, the antagonism between production and exchange is to be attenuated by the cessation of crises and the formation of capitalist employers' organizations. The antagonism between capital and labor is to be adjusted by bettering the situation of the workers and by conserving the middle classes. And the contradiction between the class state and society is to be lessened through increased state control and the progress of democracy.

It is true that the present tactic of Social Democracy does not consist in *waiting* for the antagonisms of capitalism to develop to their most extreme point and only then transforming them. On the contrary, the essence of revolutionary tactics is to recognize the *direction* of this development and then, in the political struggle, to push its consequences to the extreme. Thus, Social Democracy has combated protectionism and militarism without waiting for their reactionary character to become fully evident. Bernstein's tactics, however, are not guided by a consideration of the development and the aggravation of the contradictions of capitalism, but by the prospect of the attenuation of these contradictions. He shows this when he speaks of the "adaptation" of capitalist economy.

Now when could such a conception be correct? All the contradictions of modern society are simply the results of the capitalist process of production. If it is true that capitalism will continue to develop in the direction it has taken until the present, then its contradictions must necessarily become sharper and more aggravated instead of disappearing. The possibility of the attenuation of the contradictions of capitalism presupposes that the capitalist mode of production itself will stop its progress. In short, the general presupposition of Bernstein's theory is the *cessation of capitalist development*.

In this way, however, his theory condemns itself in a twofold manner.

In the first place, it manifests its *utopian* character in its stand on the establishment of socialism. For it is clear that a defective capitalist development cannot lead to a socialist transformation.

In the second place, Bernstein's theory reveals its *reactionary* character when it refers to the rapid capitalist development that is taking place at present. Given the development of real capitalism, how can we explain, or rather characterize, Bernstein's position?

In the first chapter, we demonstrated the untenability of the economic preconditions on which Bernstein builds his analysis of existing social relationships. We have seen that neither the credit system nor cartels can be said to be "means of adaptation" of capitalist economy. We have seen that not even the temporary cessation of crises nor the survival of the middle class can be regarded as symptoms of capitalist adaptation. But, aside from their incorrectness, there is a common characteristic in all of the above details of the theory of the means of adaptation. This theory does not seize these manifestations of contemporary economic life as they appear in their organic relationship with the whole of capitalist development, with the complete economic mechanism of capitalism. His theory pulls these details out of their living economic context. It treats them as *disjecta membra* (separate parts) of a lifeless machine.

Consider, for example, his conception of the adaptive effect of *credit*. If we recognize credit as a higher natural stage of the process of exchange and, therefore, of the contradictions inherent in capitalist exchange, we cannot at the same time see it as a mechanical means of adaptation existing outside of the process of exchange. It would be just as impossible to consider money, merchandise or capital as "means of adaptation" of capitalism.

But, no less than money, commodities and capital, credit is an organic link of capitalist economy at a certain stage of its development. Like them, it is an indispensable gear in the mechanism of capitalist economy and, at the same time, an instrument of destruction, since it aggravates the internal contradictions of capitalism.

The same thing is true of cartels and the new, perfected means of communication.

The same mechanical view is seen in the way that Bernstein describes the cessation of crises as a symptom of the "adaptation" of capitalist economy. For him, crises are simply derangements of the economic mechanism. With their cessation, he thinks, the mechanism could function smoothly. But the fact is that crises are not "derange-ments" in the usual sense of the word. They are "derangements" without which the capitalist economy as a whole could not develop at all. For if crises constitute the only method possible in capitalism — and therefore the normal method — of periodically solving the conflict between the unlimited extension of production and the narrow limits of the world market, then crises are an organic phenomenon, inseparable from capitalist economy.

In an "undisturbed" advance of capitalist production lurks a threat to capitalism that is much greater than crises. It is not the threat resulting from the contradiction between production and exchange, but from the growth of the productivity of labor itself, which leads to a constantly falling rate of profit. The fall in the rate of profit has the extremely dan-gerous tendency of rendering impossible the production of any small and middle-size capitals. It thus limits the new formation and therefore the extension of placements for capital.

And it is precisely crises that constitute the other consequence of the same process. The result of crises is the periodic *depreciation* of capital, a fall in the prices of the means of production, a paralysis of a part of the active capital, and in time the increase of profits. Crises thus create the possibilities of new investment and therefore of the advance of produc-tion. Crises therefore appear to be the instruments of rekindling the fire of capitalist development. Their cessation — not temporary cessation but their total disappearance in the world market — would not lead to the further development of the capitalist economy, as Bernstein thinks. Rather, it would drive capitalism into the swamps.

True to the mechanical view of his theory of adaptation, Bernstein forgets the necessity of crises as well as the necessity of new placements of small and middle-size capitals. And that is why the constant reap-pearance of small capital seems to him to be the sign of the cessation of capitalist development though it is, in fact, a sign of normal capitalist development.

It is important to note that there is a viewpoint from which all the above-mentioned phenomena are seen exactly as they have been presented by the theory of "adaptation." It is the viewpoint of the *individual* capitalist who reflects in his mind the economic facts around him just as they appear when deformed by the laws of competition. The isolated capitalist sees each organic part of the whole of our economy as an independent entity. He sees them as they act on him, the single capitalist. He therefore considers these facts to be simple "derangements" or simple "means of adaptation." For the isolated capitalist, it is true, crises are really simple derangements; the cessation of crises accords him a longer existence. As far as he is concerned, credit is only a means of "adapting" his insufficient productive forces to the needs of the market. And it seems to him that the cartel of which he becomes a member really suppresses industrial anarchy.

Revisionism is nothing but a theoretical generalization from the angle of the individual capitalist. Where does this viewpoint theoretically belong if not in vulgar bourgeois economics?

All the economic errors of this school rest precisely on the conception that mistakes the phenomena of competition, as seen from the angle of the individual capitalist, for the phenomena of the whole of capitalist economy. Just as Bernstein considers credit to be a means of "adaptation," so vulgar economy considers *money* to be a judicious means of "adaptation" to the needs of exchange. Vulgar economy, too, tries to find the antidote against the ills of capitalism in the phenomena of capitalism itself. Like Bernstein, it believes in the *possibility* of regulating the capitalist economy. And in the manner of Bernstein, it arrives in time at the desire to *palliate* the contradictions of capitalism, that is, at the belief in the possibility of patching up the sores of capitalism. It ends with a reactionary and not a revolutionary program. It ends up in a utopia.

The theory of revisionism can therefore be characterized in the following way. It is a theory of socialist standstill justified through a vulgar economic theory of capitalist standstill.

PART TWO:
ECONOMIC DEVELOPMENT AND SOCIALISM

The greatest conquest of the developing proletarian movement has been
the discovery of grounds of support for the realization of socialism in
the *economic relations* of capitalist society. As a result of this discovery,
socialism was changed from an "ideal" dreamed by humanity for
thousands of years to a *historical necessity*.

Bernstein denies the existence of the economic presuppositions of
socialism in the society of today. On this count his reasoning has un-
dergone an interesting evolution. At first, in the *Neue Zeit*, he simply
contested the rapidity of the process of concentration taking place in
industry. He based his position on a comparison of the occupational
statistics of Germany in 1882 and 1895. In order to use these figures
for his purpose, he was obliged to proceed in an entirely summary
and mechanical fashion. But even in the most favorable case, his reference to the persistence of middle-size enterprises could not in the least
weaken the Marxian analysis, because the latter does not presuppose,
as a condition for the realization of socialism, either a definite *rate* of
concentration of industry — that is, a definite *delay* of the realization
of socialism — or, as we have already shown, the *absolute disappearance*
of small capitals, usually described as the disappearance of the petty
bourgeoisie.

In the latest development of his ideas Bernstein furnishes us, in his
book, a new assortment of proofs: *the statistics of shareholding societies*.
These statistics are supposed to prove that the number of shareholders
increases constantly and, as a result, the capitalist class does not become
smaller but grows continually larger. It is surprising that Bernstein has
so little acquaintance with his material. And it is astonishing how poorly
he utilizes the existing data in his own behalf.

If he wanted to disprove the Marxian law of industrial development
by referring to the condition of shareholding societies, he should have
resorted to entirely different figures. Anybody who is acquainted with

the history of shareholding societies in Germany knows that their average foundation capital has *diminished* almost constantly. Thus, while before 1871 their average foundation capital reached the figure of 10.8 million marks, it was only 4.01 million marks in 1871, 3.8 million marks in 1873, less than a million from 1882 to 1887, 0.52 million in 1891 and only 0.62 million in 1892. After this date the figures oscillated around 1 million marks, falling to 1.78 million in 1895 and to 1.19 million in the course of the first half of 1897.[3]

Those are surprising figures! Using them, Bernstein hoped to show the existence of a counter-Marxian tendency for the retransformation of large enterprises into small ones. The obvious answer to his attempt is the following. If you are to prove anything by means of your statistics, you must first of all show that they refer to the same branches of industry, that the small enterprises really replace large ones, and that they do not appear only where, previously, individual enterprises, artisan industry or miniature industry were the rule. This, however, you cannot show to be true. The passage of immense shareholding societies to middle-size and small enterprises can only be explained by the fact that the system of shareholding companies continues to penetrate new branches of production. Before, only a small number of large enterprises were organized as shareholding societies. Gradually shareholding organization has won middle-size and even small enterprises. Today we can observe shareholding societies with a capital of below 1,000 marks.

Now, what is the economic significance of the ever greater extension of the system of shareholding societies? It signifies the growing socialization of production under the capitalist form — socialization not only of large but also of middle-size and small production. The extension of shareholding does not, therefore, contradict Marxist theory but, on the contrary, confirms it emphatically.

What does the economic phenomenon of a shareholding society actually amount to? It represents, on the one hand, the unification of a number of small fortunes into a large productive capital. It stands, on the other hand, for the separation of production from capitalist ownership. That is, it signifies a double victory over the capitalist mode of production — but still on a capitalist base.

What is the meaning, then, of the statistics cited by Bernstein according to which an ever greater number of shareholders participate in capitalist enterprises? These statistics demonstrate precisely the following: at present a capitalist enterprise does not correspond, as before, to a single proprietor of capital but to a number of capitalists. Consequently, the economic concept of "capitalist" no longer signifies an isolated individual. The industrial capitalist of today is a collective person composed of hundreds and even of thousands of individuals. The category "capitalist" has itself become a social category. It has become *socialized* — within the framework of capitalist society.

In that case, how shall we explain Bernstein's belief that the phenomenon of shareholding societies stands for the dispersion and not the concentration of capital? Why does he see the extension of capitalist property where Marx sees "the suppression of capitalist property"?

This is a simple, vulgar economic error. By "capitalist" Bernstein does not mean a category of production but the right to property. To him, "capitalist" is not an economic unit but a fiscal unit. And "capital" is for him not a factor of production but simply a certain quantity of money. That is why in his English sewing thread trust he does not see the fusion of 12,300 persons with money into a single capitalist unit but 12,300 different capitalists. That is why the engineer Schulze, whose wife's dowry brought him "a large number of shares" from stockholder Müller, is also a capitalist for Bernstein. That is why for Bernstein the entire world seems to swarm with capitalists.

Here, too, the theoretical base of his economic error is his "popularization" of socialism. For this is what he does. By transporting the concept of capitalism from its productive relations to property relations, and by speaking of "men instead of speaking of entrepreneurs," he moves the question of socialism from the domain of production into the domain of relations of fortune — that is, from the relation between capital and labor to the relation between poor and rich.

In this manner we are merrily led from Marx and Engels to the author of *The Evangel of the Poor Fisherman*. There is this difference, however. Weitling, with the sure instinct of the proletarian, saw in the opposition between the poor and the rich, the class antagonisms in their primitive form, and wanted to make of these a lever of the socialist movement. Bernstein, on the other hand, sees the prospects of socialism in making the poor rich, that is, in the attenuation of class antagonisms. For this reason, Bernstein is engaged in a petty-bourgeois course.

True, Bernstein does not limit himself to income statistics. He furnishes statistics of economic enterprises, and from many countries: Germany, France, England, Switzerland, Austria and the United States. But these statistics are not the comparative figures of *different periods* in each country but of each period in different countries. With the exception of Germany, where he repeats the old contrast between 1895 and 1882, we are therefore not offered a comparison of the statistics of enterprises of a given country at different epochs but the *absolute* figures for different countries: England in 1891, France in 1894, United States in 1890, etc.

He reaches the following conclusion: "Though it is true that large exploitation is already supreme in industry today, it nevertheless represents, including the enterprises dependent on it, even in a country as developed in Prussia, at most only *half* of the population occupied in production." This is also true about Germany, England, Belgium, etc.

What he proves in this way is not the existence of this or that tendency of economic development but merely the absolute relation of forces of different forms of enterprise, or put in other words, the absolute relations of the various classes in our society.

If this is supposed to prove the impossibility of realizing socialism, the reasoning must rest on the theory according to which the result of social efforts is decided by the relation of the numerical material forces of the elements in the struggle, that is, by the mere factor of *violence*. In other words, Bernstein, who always thunders against Blanquism, himself falls into the grossest Blanquist error. There is, of course, the difference that to the Blanquists, who represented a socialist and revolutionary tendency, the possibility of the economic realization of socialism appeared quite natural. On this possibility they built the chances of a violent revolution — even by a small minority. Bernstein, on the contrary, infers from the numerical insufficiency of a socialist majority, the impossibility of the economic realization of socialism. Social Democracy does not, however, expect to attain its aim either as a result of the victorious violence of a minority or through the numerical superiority of a majority. It sees socialism as a result of economic necessity — and the comprehension of that necessity — leading to the suppression of capitalism by the working masses. And this necessity manifests itself above all in the *anarchy of capitalism*.

Concerning the decisive question of anarchy in capitalist economy, Bernstein denies only the great general crises. He does not deny partial and national crises. In other words, he denies that there is a great deal of the anarchy; at the same time, he admits the existence of a little anarchy. Concerning the capitalist economy, he is — to use Marx's illustration — like the foolish virgin who had a child "who was only very small." But the misfortune is that in matters like economic anarchy, little and much are equally bad. If Bernstein recognizes the existence of a little anarchy, we may point out to him that by the mechanism of the market economy this anarchy will be extended to unheard-of proportions — to the breakdown. But if Bernstein hopes to gradually transform his bit of anarchy into order and harmony while maintaining the system of commodity production, he again falls into one of the fundamental errors of bourgeois political economy according to which the mode of exchange is treated as independent of the mode of production.

This is not the place for a detailed demonstration of Bernstein's surprising confusion concerning the most elementary principles of political economy. But there is one point — to which we are led by the fundamental questions of capitalist anarchy — that must be clarified immediately.

Bernstein declares that Marx's labor theory of value is a simple abstraction, a term which for him, obviously constitutes an insult. But if the labor theory of value is only a simple abstraction, if it is only a "mental construct" — then every normal citizen who has done military duty and pays his taxes on time has the same right as Karl Marx to fashion his favorite nonsense into such a "mental construct," to make his own law of value. "Marx has as much right to neglect the properties of commodities until they are no more than the incarnation of quantities of simple human labor as have the economists of the Böhm-Jevons school to make an abstraction of all the qualities of commodities outside of their utility."

That is, to Bernstein, Marx's social labor and Menger's abstract utility are quite similar — pure abstractions. Bernstein forgets completely that Marx's abstraction is not an invention. It is a discovery. It does not exist in Marx's head but in the commodity economy. It has not an imaginary existence but a real social existence, so real that it can be cut, hammered, weighed and coined. The abstract human labor discovered by Marx is, in its developed form, none other than *money*. That is precisely one of Marx's greatest discoveries, while to all bourgeois political economists, from the first of the mercantilists to the last of the classicists, the essence of money has remained a mystic enigma.

The Böhm-Jevons abstract utility is, in fact, a mere mental construct. Or stated more correctly, it is a construct of intellectual emptiness, a private absurdity, for which neither capitalism nor any other society can be made responsible but only vulgar bourgeois economy itself. With this "mental construct," Bernstein, Böhm and Jevons, and the entire subjective fraternity, can remain 20 years or more before the mystery of money, without arriving at a solution that is different from the one reached by any cobbler, namely that money is also a "useful" thing.

Bernstein has lost all comprehension of Marx's law of value. Anybody with a small understanding of Marxian economics can see that without the law of value, Marx's whole system is incomprehensible. Or, to speak more concretely, without an understanding of the nature of the commodity and its exchange, the entire economy of capitalism, with all its concatenations, must of necessity remain an enigma.

What precisely was the key which enabled Marx to open the door to the secrets of capitalist phenomena and solve, as if at play, problems that were not even suspected by the greatest minds of classic bourgeois economy, such as Smith and Ricardo? It was his conception of capitalist economy as a historical phenomenon — not merely, as in the best of cases by the classic economists, concerning the feudal past of capitalism, but also concerning the socialist future of the world. The secret of Marx's theory of value, of his analysis of money, of his theory of capital, of his theory of the rate of profit and consequently of the whole existing economic system is found in the transitory character of capitalist economy, the inevitability of its collapse leading — and this is only another aspect of the same phenomenon — to socialism. It is precisely because Marx looked at capitalism from the socialist's viewpoint, that is, from the historical viewpoint, that he was enabled to decipher the hieroglyphics of capitalist economy. And it is precisely because he took the socialist viewpoint as a point of departure for his analysis of bourgeois society that he was in the position to give a scientific base to the socialist movement.

This is the measure by which we evaluate Bernstein's remarks. He complains of the "dualism" found everywhere in Marx's monumental work *Capital*. "The dualism is found in that the work wishes to be a scientific study and prove, at the same time, a thesis that was completely elaborated a long time before; it is based on a schema that already contains the result to which he wants to lead. The return to *The Communist Manifesto* (that is, to the socialist goal! — R.L.), proves the existence of vestiges of utopianism in Marx's system."

But what is Marx's "dualism" if not the dualism of the socialist future and the capitalist present? It is the dualism of capital and labor, of the bourgeoisie and the proletariat. It is the monumental scientific reflection of the dualism existing in bourgeois society, the dualism of the bourgeois class antagonisms.

Bernstein's recognition of Marx's theoretical dualism as "a survival of utopianism" is really his naïve avowal that he denies the historical dualism of bourgeois society, the existence of class antagonisms in capitalism. It is his confession that socialism has become for him only a "survival of utopianism." What is Bernstein's "monism" — that is, his unity — but the eternal unity of the capitalist order, the unity of the former socialist who has renounced his aim and has decided to see in bourgeois society, one and immutable, the goal of human development?

Bernstein does not see in the economic structure of capitalism the duality, the development that leads to socialism. But in order to conserve his socialist program, at least in form, he is obliged to take refuge in an idealist construction placed outside of all economic development. He is obliged to transform socialism itself from a definite historical phase of social development into an abstract "principle."

That is why the "cooperative principle" — the meager decantation of socialism with which Bernstein wishes to garnish capitalist economy — appears as a concession made not to the socialist future of society but to Bernstein's own socialist past.

Trade Unions, Cooperatives and Political Democracy

Bernstein's socialism offers to the workers the prospect of sharing in the wealth of society. The poor are to become rich. How will this socialism be brought about? His article in the *Neue Zeit* ("Problems of Socialism") contains only vague allusions to this question. Adequate information, however, can be found in his book.

Bernstein's socialism is to be realized with the aid of these two instruments: labor unions — or as Bernstein himself characterizes them, economic democracy — and cooperatives. The first will suppress industrial profit; the second will do away with commercial profit.

Cooperatives — especially cooperatives in the field of production constitute a hybrid form in the midst of capitalism. They can be described as small units of socialized production within capitalist exchange.

But in capitalist economy exchange dominates production. As a result of competition, the complete domination of the process of production by the interests of capital — that is, pitiless exploitation — becomes a condition for the survival of each enterprise. The domination of capital over the process of production expresses itself in the following ways. Labor is intensified. The work day is lengthened or shortened, according to the situation of the market. And, depending on the requirements of the market, labor is either employed or thrown back into the street. In other words, use is made of all methods that enable an enterprise to stand up against its competitors in the market. The workers forming a cooperative in the field of production are thus faced with the contradictory necessity of governing themselves with the utmost absolutism. They are obliged to take toward themselves the role of capitalist entrepreneur — a contradiction that accounts for the usual failure of production cooperatives which either become pure capitalist enterprises or, if the workers' interests continue to predominate, end by dissolving.

Bernstein has himself taken note of these facts. But it is evident that he has not understood them. For, together with Mrs. Potter-Webb, he explains the failure of production cooperatives in England by their lack of "discipline." But what is so superficially and flatly called here "discipline" is nothing else than the natural absolutist regime of capitalism which, it is plain, the workers cannot successfully use against themselves.

Producers' cooperatives can survive within capitalist economy only if they manage to suppress, by means of some detour, the capitalist controlled contradictions between the mode of production and the mode of exchange. And they can accomplish this only by removing themselves artificially from the influence of the laws of free competition. And they can succeed in doing the last only when they assure themselves beforehand of a constant circle of consumers, that is, when they assure themselves of a constant market.

It is the consumers' cooperative that can offer this service to its brother in the field of production. Here — and not in Oppenheimer's distinction between cooperatives that produce and cooperatives that sell — is the secret sought by Bernstein: the explanation for the invariable failure of producers' cooperatives functioning independently and their survival when they are backed by consumers' organizations.

If it is true that the possibilities of existence of producers' cooperatives within capitalism are bound up with the possibilities of existence of consumers' cooperatives, then the scope of the former is limited, in the most favorable of cases, to the small local market and to the manufacture of articles serving immediate needs, especially food products. Consumers' and therefore producers' cooperatives, are excluded from the most important branches of capital production — the textile, mining, metallurgical and petroleum industries, machine construction, locomotive and shipbuilding. For this reason alone (forgetting for the moment their hybrid character), cooperatives in the field of production cannot be seriously considered as the instrument of a general social transformation. The establishment of producers' cooperatives on a wide scale would suppose, first of all, the suppression of the world market, the breaking up of the present world economy into small local spheres of production and exchange. The highly developed, widespread capitalism of our time is expected to fall back to the merchant economy of the Middle Ages.

Within the framework of present society, producers' cooperatives are limited to the role of simple annexes to consumers' cooperatives. It appears, therefore, that the latter must be the beginning of the proposed social change. But this way the expected reform of society by means of cooperatives ceases to be an offensive against capitalist production. That is, it ceases to be an attack against the principal bases of capitalist economy. It becomes, instead, a struggle against commercial capital, especially small and middle-size commercial capital. It becomes an attack made on the twigs of the capitalist tree. According to Bernstein, trade unions too are a means of attack against capitalism in the field of production. We have already shown that trade unions cannot give the workers a determining influence over production. Trade unions can determine neither the dimensions of production nor the technical progress of production.

This much may be said about the purely economic side of the "struggle of the rate of wages against the rate of profit," as Bernstein labels the activity of the trade union. It does not take place in the blue of the sky. It takes place within the well-defined framework of the law of wages. The law of wages is not shattered by applied trade union activity.

According to Bernstein, it is the trade unions that lead — in the general movement for the emancipation of the working class — the real attack against the rate of industrial profit. According to Bernstein, trade unions have the task of transforming the rate of industrial profit into "rates of wages." The fact is that trade unions are least able to execute an economic offensive against profit. Trade unions are nothing more than the organized *defense* of labor power against the attacks of profit. They express the resistance offered by the working class to the oppression of capitalist economy.

On the one hand, trade unions have the function of influencing the situation in the labor-power market. But this influence is being constantly overcome by the proletarianization of the middle layers of our society, a process which continually brings new merchandise onto the labor market. The second function of the trade unions is to ameliorate the condition of the workers. That is, they attempt to increase the share of the social wealth going to the working class. This share, however, is being reduced with the fatality of a natural process by the growth of the productivity of labor. One does not need to be a Marxist to notice this. It suffices to read Rodbertus' *In Explanation of the Social Question*.

In other words, the objective conditions of capitalist society transform the two economic functions of the trade unions into a sort of labor of Sisyphus,[4] which is, nevertheless, indispensable. For as a result of the activity of his trade unions, the worker succeeds in obtaining for himself the rate of wages due to him in accordance with the situation of the labor-power market. As a result of trade union activity, the capitalist law of wages is applied and the effect of the depressing tendency of economic development is paralyzed, or to be more exact, attenuated.

However, the transformation of the trade union into an instrument for the progressive reduction of profit in favor of wages presupposes the following social conditions; first, the cessation of the proletarianization of the middle strata of our society; secondly, a stoppage of the growth of productivity of labor. We have in both cases *a return to pre-capitalist conditions.*

Cooperatives and trade unions are totally incapable of transforming the *capitalist mode of production.* This is really understood by Bernstein, though in a confused manner. For he refers to cooperatives and trade unions as a means of reducing the profit of the capitalists and thus enriching the workers. In this way, he renounces the struggle against the *capitalist mode of production* and attempts to direct the socialist movement to struggle against "capitalist distribution." Again and again, Bernstein refers to socialism as an effort toward a "just, juster and still more just" mode of distribution.[5]

It cannot be denied that the direct cause leading the popular masses into the socialist movement is precisely the "unjust" mode of distribution characteristic of capitalism. When Social Democracy struggles for the socialization of the entire economy, it aspires there-with also to a "just" distribution of the social wealth. But, guided by Marx's observation that the mode of distribution of a given epoch is a natural consequence of the mode of production of that epoch, Social Democracy does not struggle against distribution in the framework of capitalist production. It struggles instead for the suppression of the capitalist production itself. In a word, Social Democracy wants to establish the mode of socialist distribution by suppressing the capitalist mode of production. Bernstein's method, on the contrary, proposes to combat the capitalist mode of distribution in the hopes of gradually establishing, in this way, the socialist mode of production.

What, in that case, is the basis of Bernstein's program for the reform of society? Does it find support in definite tendencies of capitalist production? No. In the first place, he denies such tendencies. In the second place, the socialist transformation of production is for him the effect and not the cause of distribution. He cannot give his program a materialist base, because he has already overthrown the aims and the means of the movement for socialism, and therefore its economic conditions. As a result, he is obliged to construct himself an idealist base.

"Why represent socialism as the consequence of economic compulsion?" he complains. "Why degrade man's understanding, his feeling for justice, his will?"[6] Bernstein's superlatively just distribution is to be attained thanks to man's free will; man's will acting not because of economic necessity, since this will is only an instrument, but because of man's comprehension of justice, because of man's *idea of justice.*

We thus quite happily return to the principle of justice, to the old war horse on which the reformers of the earth have rocked for ages, for the lack of surer means of historical transportation. We return to the lamentable Rosinante on which the Don Quixotes of history have galloped toward the great reform of the earth, always to come home with their eyes blackened.

The relation of the poor to the rich, taken as a base for socialism, the principle of cooperation as the content of socialism, the "most just distribution" as its aim, and the idea of justice as its only historical legitimization — with how much more force and fire did Weitling defend that sort of socialism 50 years ago. However, that genius of a tailor did not know scientific socialism. If today, the conception tore into bits by Marx and Engels half a century ago is patched up and presented to the proletariat as the last world of social science, that, too, is the art of a tailor but it has nothing of a genius about it.

Trade unions and cooperatives are the economic support for the theory of revisionism. Its principal political condition is the growth of democracy. The present manifestations of political reaction are to Bernstein only "displacement." He considers them accidental, momentary, and suggests that they are not to be considered in the elaboration of the general directives of the labor movement.

According to Bernstein, democracy is an inevitable stage in the development of society. To him, as to the bourgeois theoreticians of liberalism, democracy is the great fundamental law of historical development, the realization of which is served by all the forces of political life. However, Bernstein's thesis is completely false. Presented in this absolute form, it is a petty-bourgeois vulgarization of results of a very short phase of bourgeois development, the last 25 or 30 years. We reach entirely different conclusions when we examine the historical development of democracy and consider, at the same time, the general political history of capitalism.

Democracy has been found in the most dissimilar social formations: in primitive communist societies, in the slave states of antiquity and in medieval communes. Similarly, absolutism and constitutional monarchy are to be found under the most varied economic orders. When capitalism began, with the first production of commodities, it resorted to a democratic constitution in the municipal-communes of the Middle Ages. Later, when it developed to manufacturing, capitalism found its corresponding political form in the absolute monarchy. Finally, as a developed industrial economy, it brought into being in France the democratic Republic of 1793, the absolute monarchy of Napoleon I, the nobles' monarchy of the Restoration period (1815–30), the bourgeois constitutional monarchy of Louis-Philippe, then again the democratic Republic, and again the monarchy of Napoleon III, and finally, for the third time, the Republic. In Germany, the only truly democratic institution — universal suffrage — is not a conquest won by bourgeois liberalism. Universal suffrage in Germany was an instrument for the fusion of the small states. It is only in this sense that it has any importance for the development of the German bourgeoisie, which is otherwise quite satisfied with a semifeudal constitutional monarchy. In Russia, capitalism prospered for a long time under the regime of oriental personal rule, without the bourgeoisie manifesting the least desire to introduce democracy. In Austria, universal suffrage was above all a life line thrown to a foundering and decomposing monarchy. In Belgium, the conquest of universal suffrage by the labor movement was undoubtedly due to the weakness of local militarism, and consequently to the special geographic and political situation of the country. But we have here a "bit of democracy" that has been won not *by* the bourgeoisie but *against it.*

The uninterrupted ascent of democracy, which to our revisionism as well as to bourgeois liberalism appears as a great fundamental law of human history and, especially, modern history, is shown upon closer examination to be a phantom. No absolute and general relation can be constructed between capitalist development and democracy. The political form of a given country is always the result of the whole sum of political factors, domestic as well as foreign. It admits within its limits all variations of scale from absolute monarchy to the democratic republic.

We must therefore abandon all hope of establishing democracy as a general law of historical development even within the framework of modern society. Turning to the present phase of bourgeois society, we observe here, too, political factors which, instead of assuring the realization of Bernstein's schema, lead rather to the abandonment by bourgeois society of the democratic conquests won up to now.

Democratic institutions — and this is of the greatest significance — have completely exhausted their function as aids in the development of bourgeois society. Insofar as they were necessary to bring about the fusion of small states and the creation of large modern states (Germany, Italy), they have become dispensable. Economic development has meanwhile effected an internal organic healing.

The same thing can be said concerning the transformation of the entire political and administrative state machinery from a feudal or semi-feudal mechanism to a capitalist mechanism. While this transformation has been historically inseparable from the development of democracy, it has been realized today to such an extent that the purely democratic "ingredients" of society, such as universal suffrage and the republican state form, may be suppressed without having the administration, the state finances, or the military organization find it necessary to return to the forms they had before the March Revolution.[7]

If liberalism as such is now absolutely useless to bourgeois society, it has become, on the other hand, a direct impediment. Two factors completely dominate the political life of contemporary states: *world politics* and the labor movement. Each is only a different aspect of the present phase of capitalist development.

As a result of the development of the world economy and the aggravation and generalization of competition on the world market, militarism and the policy of large navies have become, as instruments of world politics, a decisive factor in the internal as well as in the external life of the great states. If it is true that world politics and militarism represent a *rising* tendency in the present phase of capitalism, then bourgeois democracy must logically move in a *descending* line.

In Germany, the new era of great armaments (1893) and that of world politics, inaugurated with the seizure of Kiao-Cheou, were paid for immediately with the following sacrificial victims: the decomposition of liberalism and the deflation of the Center Party, which passed from opposition to government. The recent elections to the Reichstag of 1907 unrolling under the sign of the German colonial policy were, at the same time, the historical burial of German liberalism.

If foreign policy pushes the bourgeoisie into the arms of reaction this is no less true of domestic politics — thanks to the rise of the working class. Bernstein shows that he recognizes this when he makes the "legend" of Social Democracy which "wants to swallow everything" — in other words, the socialist efforts of the working class — responsible for the desertion of the liberal bourgeoisie. He advises the proletariat to disavow its socialist aim so that the mortally frightened liberals might come out of the mousehole of reaction. Making the abandonment of the socialist labor movement an essential condition for the preservation of bourgeois democracy, he proves in a striking manner that this democracy is in complete contradiction with the inner tendency of development of modern society. He proves, at the same time, that the socialist movement is itself a *direct product* of this tendency.

But he proves, at the same time, still another thing. By making the renunciation of the socialist goal an essential condition of the resurrection of bourgeois democracy, he shows how inexact is the claim that bourgeois democracy is an indispensable condition of the socialist movement and the victory of socialism. Bernstein's reasoning exhausts itself in a vicious circle. His conclusion swallows his premises.

The exit from this circle is quite simple. In view of that fact that bourgeois liberalism has sold its soul from fear of the growing labor movement and its final aim, it follows that the socialist labor movement today is and can be the *only* support of democracy. The fate of the socialist movement is not bound to bourgeois democracy; but the fate of democracy, on the contrary, is bound to the socialist movement. Democracy does not acquire greater chances of life in the measure that the working class renounces the struggle for its emancipation; on the contrary, democracy acquires greater chances of survival as the socialist movement becomes sufficiently strong to struggle against the reactionary consequences of world politics and the bourgeois desertion of democracy. He who would strengthen democracy must also want to strengthen and not weaken the socialist movement; and with the renunciation of the struggle for socialism goes that of both the labor movement and democracy.

The Conquest of Political Power

The fate of democracy is bound up, as we have seen, with the fate of the labor movement. But does the development of democracy render superfluous or impossible a proletarian revolution, that is, the conquest of political power by the workers?

Bernstein settles the question by weighing minutely the good and bad sides of social reform and social revolution. He does it almost in the same manner in which cinnamon or pepper is weighed out in a consumers' cooperative store. He sees the legislative course of historical development as the action of "intelligence," while the revolutionary course of historical development is for him the action of "feeling." Reformist activity he recognizes as a slow method of historical progress, revolution as a rapid method of progress. In legislation he sees a methodical force; in revolution, a spontaneous force.

We have known for a long time that the petty-bourgeois reformer finds "good" and "bad" sides in everything. He nibbles a bit at all grasses. But the real course of events is little affected by such petty-bourgeois combinations. The carefully gathered little pile of the "good sides" of all things possible blows away at the first wind of history. Historically, legislative reform and the revolutionary method function in accordance with influences that are much more profound than the consideration of the advantages or inconveniences of one method or another.

In the history of bourgeois society, legislative reform served to progressively strengthen the rising class until the latter felt sufficiently strong to seize political power, to overturn the existing juridical system and to construct itself a new one. Bernstein, thundering against the conquest of political power as a theory of Blanquist violence, has the misfortune of labeling as a Blanquist error that which for centuries has been the pivot and the motive force of human history. As long as class societies have existed, and the class struggle has constituted the essential content of their history, the conquest of political power has been the aim of all rising classes, and the starting point and end of every historical period. This can be seen in the long struggle of the peasantry against the financiers and nobility of ancient Rome; in the struggle of the medieval nobility against the bishops, and the artisans against the nobles in the cities of the Middle Ages; and in modern times, in the struggle of the bourgeoisie against feudalism.

Legal reform and revolution are not different methods of historical progress that can be picked out at pleasure from the counter of history, just as one chooses hot or cold sausages. They are different *moments* in the development of class society which condition and complement each other, and at the same time exclude each other reciprocally as, e.g., the north and south poles, the bourgeoisie and proletariat.

In effect, every legal constitution is the *product* of a revolution. In the history of classes, revolution is the act of political creation while legislation is the political expression of the life of a society that has already come into being. Work for legal reforms does not itself contain its own driving force independent from revolution. During every historical period, work for reforms is carried on only in the direction given to it by the impetus of the last revolution and continues as long as the impulsion from the last revolution continues to make itself felt. Or, to put it more concretely, in each historical period work for reforms is carried on only in the framework of the social form created by the last revolution. Here is the kernel of the problem.

It is absolutely false and totally unhistorical to represent work for reforms as a drawn-out revolution, and revolution as a condensed series of reforms. A social transformation and a legislative reform do not differ according to their *duration* but according to their *essence*. The secret of historical change through the utilization of political power resides precisely in the transformation of simple quantitative modification into a new quality, or to speak more concretely, in the transition from one historical period, one social order, to another.

That is why people who pronounce themselves in favor of the method of legislative reform *in place of and as opposed to* the conquest of political power and social revolution, do not really choose a more tranquil, calmer and slower road to the *same* goal. They choose a *different* goal. Instead of taking a stand for the establishment of a new society they take a stand for surface modifications of the old society.

If we follow the political conceptions of revisionism, we arrive at the same conclusion that is reached when we follow the economic theories of revisionism. The program becomes not the realization of *socialism*, but the reform of *capitalism*; not the suppression of the wage labor system but the diminution of exploitation, that is, the suppression of the abuses of capitalism instead of capitalism itself.

Does the reciprocal role of legislative reform and revolution apply only to the class struggle of the past? It is possible that now, as a result of the development of the bourgeois juridical system, the function of moving society from one historical phase to another belongs to legislative reform and that the conquest of state power by the proletariat has really become "an empty phrase," as Bernstein puts it?

The very opposite is true. What distinguishes bourgeois society from other class societies — from ancient society and from the social order of the Middle Ages? Precisely the fact that class domination does not rest on "acquired rights" but on *real economic relations* — the fact that wage labor is not a juridical relation, but purely an economic relation. In our juridical system there is not a single legal formula for the class domination of today. The few remaining traces of such formulae of class domination are (as that concerning servants), survivals of feudal society.

How can wage slavery be suppressed the "legislative way," if wage slavery is not expressed in the laws? Bernstein, who would do away with capitalism by means of legislative reforms, finds himself in the same situation as Uspensky's Russian policeman who said: "Quickly! I seized the rascal by the collar! But what do I see? The confounded fellow has no collar!" And that is precisely Bernstein's difficulty.

"Every form of society has been based... on the antagonism of oppressing and oppressed classes."[8] But in the preceding phases of modern society, this antagonism was expressed in distinctly determined juridical relations and could, especially because of that, accord, to a certain extent, a place to new relations within the framework of the old. "The serf, in the period of serfdom, raised himself to membership in the commune."[9] How was that made possible? It was made possible by the progressive suppression of all feudal privileges in the environs of the city: the corvee, the right to special dress, the inheritance tax, the lord's claim to the best cattle, the personal levy, marriage under duress, the right to succession, etc., which all together constituted serfdom.

In the same way, the small bourgeoisie of the Middle Ages succeeded in raising itself, while it was still under the yoke of feudal absolutism, to the rank of bourgeoisie.[10] By what means? By means of the formal partial suppression or complete loosening of the corporative bonds, by the progressive transformation of the fiscal administration and of the army.

Consequently, when we consider the question from the abstract viewpoint, not from the historical viewpoint, we can *imagine* (in view of the former class relations) a legal passage, according to the reformist method, from feudal society to bourgeois society. But what do we see in reality? In reality, we see that legal reforms not only do not obviate the seizure of political power by the bourgeoisie but have, on the contrary, prepared for it and led to it. A formal social-political transformation was indispensable for the abolition of slavery as well as for the complete suppression of feudalism.

But the situation is entirely different now. No law obliges the proletariat to submit itself to the yoke of capitalism. Poverty, the lack of means of production, obliges the proletariat to submit itself to the yoke of capitalism. And no law in the world can give to the proletariat the means of production while it remains in the framework of bourgeois society, for not laws but economic development have torn the means of production from the producers' possession.

And neither is the exploitation inside the system of wage labor based on laws. The level of wages is not fixed by legislation but by economic factors. The phenomenon of capitalist exploitation does not rest on a legal disposition but on the purely economic fact that labor power plays in this exploitation the role of a merchandise possessing, among other characteristics, the agreeable quality of producing value — *more* than the value it consumes in the form of the laborer's means of subsistence. In short, the fundamental relations of the domination of the capitalist class cannot be transformed by means of legislative reforms, on the basis of capitalist society, because these relations have not been introduced by bourgeois laws, nor have they received the form of such laws. Apparently, Bernstein is not aware of this for he speaks of "socialist reforms." On the other hand, he seems to express implicit recognition of this when he writes, on page 10 of his book, "the economic motive acts freely today, while formerly it was masked by all kinds of relations of domination by all sorts of ideology."

It is one of the peculiarities of the capitalist order that within it all the elements of the future society first assume, in their development, a form not approaching socialism but, on the contrary, a form moving more and more away from socialism. Production takes on a progressively increasing social character. But under what form is the social character of capitalist production expressed? It is expressed in the form of the large enterprise, in the form of the shareholding concern, the cartel, within which the capitalist antagonisms, capitalist exploitation, the oppression of labor power, are augmented to the extreme.

In the army, capitalist development leads to the extension of obligatory military service, to the reduction of the time of service and consequently to a material approach to a popular militia. But all of this takes place under the form of modern militarism in which the domination of the people by the militarist state and the class character of the state manifest themselves most clearly.

In the field of political relations, the development of democracy brings — in the measure that it finds a favorable soil — the participation of all popular strata in political life and, consequently, some sort of "people's state." But this participation takes the form of bourgeois parliamentarism, in which class antagonisms and class domination are not done away with, but are, on the contrary, displayed in the open. Exactly because capitalist development moves through these contradictions, it is necessary to extract the kernel of socialist society from its capitalist shell. Exactly for this reason must the proletariat seize political power and suppress completely the capitalist system.

Of course, Bernstein draws other conclusions. If the development of democracy leads to the aggravation and not to the lessening of capitalist antagonisms, "Social Democracy," he answers us, "in order not to render its task more difficult, must by all means try to stop social reforms and the extension of democratic institutions." Indeed, that would be the right thing to do if Social Democracy found to its taste, in the petty-bourgeois manner, the futile task of picking for itself all the good sides of history and rejecting the bad sides of history. However, in that case, it should at the same time "try to stop" capitalism in general, for there is no doubt that latter is the rascal placing all these obstacles in the way of socialism. But capitalism furnishes besides the *obstacles* also the only *possibilities* of realizing the socialist program. The same can be said about democracy.

If democracy has become superfluous or annoying to the bourgeoisie, it is on the contrary necessary and indispensable to the working class. It is necessary to the working class because it creates the political forms (autonomous administration, electoral rights, etc.) which will serve the proletariat as fulcrums in its task of transforming bourgeois society. Democracy is indispensable to the working class because only through the exercise of its democratic rights, in the struggle for democracy, can the proletariat become aware of its class interests and its historical task.

In a word, democracy is indispensable not because it renders superfluous the conquest of political power by the proletariat but because it renders this conquest of power both *necessary* and *possible*. When Engels, in his preface to *The Class Struggles in France*, revised the tactics of the modern labor movement and urged the legal struggle as opposed to the barricades, he did not have in mind — *this comes out of every line of the preface* — the question of the final conquest of political power, but the modern daily struggle; not the attitude of the proletariat *opposed* to the capitalist state at the moment of the seizure of power but its attitude within the *bounds* of the capitalist state. Engels gave directions to the *oppressed* proletariat, not to the victorious proletariat.

On the other hand, Marx's well-known sentence on the agrarian question in England, on which Bernstein leans heavily — "We would probably succeed more easily by buying out the landlords" — does not refer to the attitude of the proletariat *before* but *after its victory*. For there evidently can be a question of buying the property of the old dominant class only when the workers are in power. The possibility envisaged by Marx is that of the *peaceful exercise of the dictatorship of the proletariat* and not the replacement of the dictatorship by capitalist social reforms. There was no doubt for Marx and Engels about the necessity of the proletariat conquering political power. It is left to Bernstein to consider the poultry-yard of bourgeois parliamentarism as the organ by means of which the most formidable social transformation of history, the passage of society from the *capitalist* to the *socialist* form, is to be completed.

Bernstein introduces his theory by warning the proletariat against the danger of acquiring power too *early*! That is, according to Bernstein, the proletariat ought to leave the bourgeois society in its present condition and itself suffer a frightful defeat. If the proletariat came to power, it could draw from Bernstein's theory the following "practical" conclusion: to go to sleep. His theory condemns the proletariat at the most decisive moments of the struggle, to inactivity, to a passive betrayal of its own cause.

Our program would be a miserable scrap of paper if it could not serve us in *all* eventualities, at *all* moments of the struggle, and serve precisely by its *application* and not by its nonapplication. If our program contains the formula of the historical development of society from capitalism to socialism, it must also formulate, in all its characteristic fundamentals, all the transitory phases of this development and it should, consequently, be able to indicate to the proletariat what ought to be its corresponding action at every moment on the road toward socialism. There can be *no time* for the proletariat when it will be obliged to abandon its program, or be abandoned by it.

Practically, this is manifested in the fact that there can be no time when the proletariat, placed in power by the force of events, is not in the condition or is not morally obliged to take certain measures for the realization of its program, that is, to take transitory measures in the direction of socialism. Behind the belief that the socialist program could break down at any moment during the political domination of the proletariat, and give no directions for its realization, lies, unconsciously, the other belief, that the *socialist program is generally and at all times, unrealizable.*

And what if the transitory measures are premature? The question hides a great number of mistaken ideas concerning the real course of social transformations.

In the first place, the seizure of political power by the proletariat, that is to say, by a large popular class, is not produced artificially. It presupposes (with the exception of cases like the Paris Commune, when power was not obtained after a conscious struggle for its goal, but, exceptionally, fell into the proletariat's hands like an object abandoned by everybody else) a definite degree of maturity of economic and political relations. Here we have the essential difference between Blanquist *coups d'état* by a "resolute minority," bursting out like pistol shot, and always inopportunely, and the conquest of political power by a large and class-conscious popular mass. Such a mass itself can only be the product of the decomposition of bourgeois society and therefore bears in itself the economic and political legitimization of its opportune appearance.

If, therefore, considered from the standpoint of the social presuppositions, the conquest of political power by the working class cannot occur "too early," then from the standpoint of political effect — of *conservation* of power — it is necessarily "too early." The premature revolution, the thought of which keeps Bernstein awake, menaces us like a sword of Damocles. Against that neither prayers nor supplication, neither scares nor any amount of anguish, are of any avail. And this, for two very simple reasons.

In the first place, it is impossible to imagine that a transformation as formidable as the passage from capitalist society to socialist society can be realized in one act, by a victorious blow of the proletariat. To consider that as possible is, again, to lend credence to conceptions that are clearly Blanquist. The socialist transformation presupposes a long and stubborn struggle in the course of which, quite probably, the proletariat will be repulsed more than once so that, from the standpoint of the final outcome of the struggle, it will have necessarily come to power "too early" for the first time.

In the second place, it will be impossible to avoid the "premature" conquest of state power by the proletariat precisely because these "premature" attacks of the proletariat constitute a factor, and indeed a very important factor, creating the *political* conditions of the final victory. In the course of the political crisis accompanying its seizure of power, in the course of the long and stubborn struggles, the proletariat will acquire the degree of political maturity permitting it to obtain in time a definitive victory of the revolution. Thus these "premature" attacks of the proletariat against the state power are in themselves important historical moments helping to provoke and determine the *point* of the definite victory. Considered from *this* view-point, the idea of a "premature" conquest of political power by the laboring class appears to be a political absurdity, derived from a mechanical conception of the development of society, and positing for the victory of the class struggle a point fixed *outside* and *independent* of the class struggle.

Since the proletariat is not in the position to seize power in any other way than "prematurely," since the proletariat is absolutely obliged to seize power "too early" once or several times before it can enduringly maintain itself in power, the objection to the "premature" conquest of power is at bottom nothing more than a *general opposition to the aspiration of the proletariat to possess itself of state power*. Just as all roads lead to Rome so, too, do we logically arrive at the conclusion that the revisionist proposal to abandon the ultimate goal of socialism is really a recommendation to renounce the socialist *movement* itself.

The Breakdown

Bernstein began his revision of Social Democracy by abandoning the theory of capitalist breakdown. The latter, however, is the cornerstone of scientific socialism. By rejecting it Bernstein also rejects the whole doctrine of socialism. In the course of his discussion, he abandons, one after another, the positions of socialism in order to be able to maintain his first affirmation.

Without the breakdown of capitalism the expropriation of the capitalist class is impossible. Bernstein therefore renounces expropriation and chooses a progressive realization of the "cooperative principle" as the aim of the labor movement.

But cooperation cannot be realized without capitalist production. Bernstein therefore renounces the socialization of production and merely proposes to reform commerce and to develop consumers' cooperatives.

But the transformation of society through consumers' cooperatives, even by means of trade unions, is incompatible with the real material development of capitalist society. Therefore, Bernstein abandons the materialist conception of history.

But his conception of the march of economic development is incompatible with the Marxist theory of surplus value. Therefore, Bernstein abandons the theory of value and of surplus value and, in this way, the whole economic theory of Karl Marx.

But the class struggle of the proletariat cannot be carried on without a definite final aim and without an economic base in the existing society. Bernstein, therefore, abandons the class struggle and proclaims the reconciliation with bourgeois liberalism.

But in a class society, the class struggle is a natural and unavoidable phenomenon. Bernstein, therefore, contests even the existence of classes in society. The working class is for him a mass of individuals, divided not only politically and intellectually but also economically. And the bourgeoisie, according to him, does not group itself politically in accordance with its inner economic interest, but only because of external pressure, from above and below.

But if there is no economic base for the class struggle and, if consequently, there are no classes in our society, not only the future but even the past struggles of the proletariat against the bourgeoisie appear to be impossible and Social Democracy and its successes seem absolutely incomprehensible. Or, they can be understood only as the results of political pressure by the government — that is, not as the natural consequence of historical development but as the fortuitous consequences of the policy of the Hohenzollern; not as the legitimate offspring of capitalist society but as the bastard children of reaction. Rigorously logical, in this respect, Bernstein passes from the materialist conception of history to the outlook of the *Frankfurter Zeitung* and the *Vossische Zeitung*.

After rejecting the socialist criticism of capitalist society, it is easy for Bernstein to find the present state of affairs satisfactory — at least in a general way. Bernstein does not hesitate. He finds that at present the reaction is not very strong in Germany, that "we cannot speak of political reaction in the countries of western Europe," and that in all the countries of the West "the attitude of the bourgeois classes toward the socialist movement is at most an attitude of defence but not one of oppression."[11] Far from becoming worse, the situation of the workers is getting better. Indeed, the bourgeoisie is politically progressive and morally healthy. We cannot speak either of reaction or oppression. It is all for the best in the best of all possible worlds...

Bernstein thus travels in logical sequence from A to Z. He began by abandoning the *final aim* in favor of the movement. But as there can be no socialist movement without a socialist aim he ends by renouncing the *movement* itself.

And thus Bernstein's conception of socialism collapses entirely. The proud and admirable symmetric construction of the Marxist system becomes for him a pile of rubbish in which the debris of all systems, the pieces of thought of various great and small minds, find a common grave. Marx and Proudhon, Leon von Buch and Franz Oppenheimer, Friedrich Albert Lange and Kant, Herr Prokopovich and Dr. Ritter von Neupauer, Herkner and Schulze-Gaevernitz, Lassalle and Professor Julius Wolff: all contribute something to Bernstein's system. From each he takes a little. This is not astonishing. For when he abandoned scientific socialism he lost the axis of intellectual crystallization around which isolated facts group themselves in the organic whole of a coherent conception of the world.

His doctrine, composed of bits of all possible systems, seems on first consideration to be completely free from prejudices. For Bernstein does not like talk of "party science," or to be more exact, of class science, any more than he likes to talk of class liberalism or class morality. He thinks he succeeds in expressing a universal human abstract science, abstract liberalism, abstract morality. But since the actual society is made up of classes which have diametrically opposed interests, aspirations and conceptions, a universal human science in social questions, an abstract liberalism, an abstract morality, are at present illusions, a self-deception. What Bernstein considers his universal human science, democracy and morality, is merely the dominant science, dominant democracy and dominant morality, that is, bourgeois science, bourgeois democracy, bourgeois morality.

When Bernstein rejects the economic doctrine of Marx in order to swear by the teachings of Bretano, Böhm-Jevons, Say and Julius Wolff, he exchanges the scientific base of the emancipation of the working class for the apologetics of the bourgeoisie. When he speaks of the universal human character of liberalism and transforms socialism into a variety of liberalism, he deprives the socialist movement (generally) of its class character and consequently of its historical content, and consequently of all content; conversely, he recognizes the class representing liberalism in history, the bourgeoisie, as the champion of the universal interests of humanity.

And when he condemns the "raising of the material factors to the rank of an all-powerful force of development"; when he protests against the so-called "contempt for the ideal" that is supposed to rule Social Democracy; when he presumes to talk for idealism, for morals, pronouncing himself at the same time against the only source of the moral rebirth of the proletariat, a revolutionary class struggle — he does no more than preach to the working class the quintessence of the morality of the bourgeoisie, that is, reconciliation with the existing social order and the transfer of hope to the beyond of an ethical ideal-world.

When he directs his keenest arrows against our dialectic system, he is really attacking the specific mode of thought employed by the conscious proletariat in its struggle for liberation. It is an attempt to break the sword that has helped the proletariat pierce the darkness of its future. It is an attempt to shatter the intellectual weapon with the aid of which the proletariat, though materially under the yoke of the bourgeoisie, is yet enabled to triumph over the bourgeoisie. For it is our dialectical system that shows to the working class the transitory nature of this yoke, proving to workers the inevitability of their victory and is already realizing a revolution in the domain of thought. Saying goodbye to our system of dialectics and resorting instead to the intellectual seesaw of the well-known "on the one hand, on the other hand," "yes, but," "although, however," "more, less," etc., he quite logically lapses into the historically conditioned mode of thought of the declining bourgeoisie, a mode of thought which is the faithful intellectual reflection of its social existence and political activity. The political "on the one hand, on the other hand," "yes, but" of the bourgeoisie of today exactly resembles Bernstein's manner of thinking. This is the sharpest and surest symptom of his bourgeois conception of the world.

But, as it is used by Bernstein, the word "bourgeois" itself is not a class expression but a general social notion. Logical to the end, he has exchanged, together with his science, politics, morals and mode of thinking, the historic language of the proletariat for that of the bourgeoisie.

When he uses, without distinction, the term "citizen" in reference to the bourgeois as well as to the proletarian, thus intending to refer to man in general, he in fact identifies man in general with the bourgeois, and human society with bourgeois society.

Opportunism in Theory and Practice

Bernstein's book is of great importance to the German and the international labor movement. It is the first attempt to give a theoretical base to the opportunist currents common in Social Democracy.

These currents may be said to have existed for a long time in our movement, if we take into consideration such sporadic manifestations of opportunism as the question of subsidies for steamships. But it is only since about 1890, with the suppression of the antisocialist laws and the reconquest of the terrain of legality, that we have had an explicit, unitary opportunist current. Vollmar's "state socialism," the vote on the Bavarian budget, the "agrarian socialism" of south Germany, Heine's policy of compensation, Schippel's stand on tariffs and militarism, are the high points in the development of the opportunist practice.

What appears to characterize this practice above all? A certain hostility to "theory." This is quite natural, for our "theory," i.e., the principles of scientific socialism, impose clearly marked limitations to practical activity — concerning the *aims* of this activity, the *means* of struggle applied and the *method* of struggle. It is quite natural for those who only run after practical results want to free their hands, i.e., to split our practice from "theory," to make it independent of "theory."

But at every practical effort, this theory hits them on the head. State socialism, agrarian socialism, the policy of compensation, the militia question, all constitute defeats of opportunism. It is clear that, if this current is to maintain itself, it must try to destroy the principles of our theory and elaborate a theory of its own. Bernstein's book is precisely an effort in that direction. That is why at the Stuttgart Party Congress all the opportunist elements in our Party immediately grouped themselves around Bernstein's banner. If the opportunist currents in the practical activity of our Party are an entirely natural phenomenon which can be explained in the light of the special conditions of our activity and its development, Bernstein's theory is no less natural an attempt to group these currents into a general theoretical expression, an attempt to elaborate its own theoretical conditions and to break with scientific socialism. Bernstein's theory is thus the theoretical ordeal by fire for opportunism, its first scientific legitimization.

What was the result of this test? We have seen the result. Opportunism is not in a position to elaborate a positive theory capable of withstanding criticism. All it can do is to attack various isolated theses of Marxist theory and, just because Marxist doctrine constitutes one solidly constructed edifice, hope by this means to shake the entire system from the top to its foundation.

This shows that opportunist practice is essentially irreconcilable with Marxism. But it also proves that opportunism is incompatible with socialism (the socialist movement) in general, that its internal tendency is to push the labor movement into bourgeois paths, that opportunism tends to paralyze completely the proletarian class struggle. The latter, considered historically, has evidently nothing to do with Marxist doctrine. For, before Marx and independently from him, there have been labor movements and various socialist doctrines, each of which, in its way, was the theoretical expression corresponding to the conditions of the time, of the struggle of the working class for emancipation. The theory that consists in basing socialism on the moral notion of justice, on a struggle against the mode of distribution, instead of basing it on a struggle against the mode of production, the conception of class antagonism as an antagonism between the poor and the rich, the effort to graft the "cooperative principle" on capitalist economy — all of what we find in Bernstein's doctrine — already existed before him. And these theories were, *in their time*, in spite of their insufficiency, effective theories of the proletarian class struggle. They were the children's seven-league boots, thanks to which the proletariat learned to walk upon the scene of history.

But *after* the development of the class struggle itself and its social conditions had led to the abandonment of these theories and to the elaboration of the principles of scientific socialism, there could be no socialism — at least in Germany — outside of Marxist socialism and there could be no socialist class struggle outside of Social Democracy. From then on, socialism and Marxism, the proletarian struggle for emancipation and Social Democracy, were identical. That is why the return to pre-Marxist socialist theories no longer signifies a return to the seven-league boots of the childhood of the proletariat, but a return to the puny, worn-out slippers of the bourgeoisie.

Bernstein's theory was the *first*, and at the same time, the *last* attempt to give a theoretical base to opportunism. It is the last, because in Bernstein's system, opportunism has gone so far — negatively, through its renunciation of scientific socialism, and positively, through its marshalling of every bit of theoretical confusion possible — that nothing remains to be done. In Bernstein's book, opportunism has completed its theoretical development (just as it completed its practical development in the position taken by Schippel on the question of militarism), and has reached its ultimate conclusion.

Marxist doctrine can not only refute opportunism theoretically. It alone can explain opportunism as a historical phenomenon in the development of the Party. The world-historical forward march of the proletariat to its final victory is not, indeed, "so simple a thing." The original character of this movement consists in the fact that here, for the first time in history, the popular masses themselves, *in opposition* to all ruling classes, impose their will. But they must posit this will outside of and beyond the present society. The masses can only form this *will* in a constant struggle against the existing order. The unification of the broad popular masses with an aim reaching beyond the existing social order, the union of the daily struggle with the great world transformation — that is the task of the Social Democratic movement, which must successfully work forward on its road to development between two reefs: abandoning the mass character of the Party or abandoning its final aim, falling into bourgeois reformism or into sectarianism, anarchism or opportunism.

In its theoretical arsenal, Marxist doctrine furnished, more than half a century ago, arms that are effective against both of these extremes. But because our movement is a mass movement and because the dangers menacing it are not derived from the human brain but from social conditions, Marxist doctrine could not assure us, in advance and once for always, against the anarchist and opportunist tendencies. The latter can be overcome only as we pass from the domain of theory to the domain of practice, but only with the help of the arms furnished us by Marx.

"Bourgeois revolutions," wrote Marx a half century ago in his *Eighteenth Brumaire of Louis Napoleon*, "like those of the 18th century, rush onward rapidly from success to success; their dramatic effects surpass one another, men and things seem to be set in flaming diamonds, ecstasy is the prevailing spirit. But they are short-lived; they reach their climax quickly, and then society relapses into a long hangover before it soberly learns how to appropriate the fruits of its period of storm and stress. Proletarian revolutions, on the contrary, such as those of the 19th century, criticize themselves continually; constantly interrupt themselves in their own course; come back to what seems to have been accomplished, in order to start anew; scorn with cruel thoroughness the half-measures, weakness and wretchedness of their first attempts; seem to throw down their adversary only to enable him to draw fresh strength from the earth and again to rise up against them, still more gigantically; constantly recoil in fear before the undefined enormity of their own goals — until the situation is created which renders all retreat impossible, and conditions themselves cry out: '*Hic Rhodus, hic salta!*' Here is the rose. Dance here!"

This has remained true even after the elaboration of the doctrine of scientific socialism. The proletarian movement has not as yet, all at once, become Social Democratic, even in Germany. But it is *becoming* more Social Democratic, continuously surmounting the extreme deviations of anarchism and opportunism, both of which are only determining phases of the development of Social Democracy, considered as a *process*.

For these reasons, we must say that the surprising thing here is not the appearance of an opportunist current but rather its weakness. As long as it showed itself in isolated cases of the practical activity of the Party, one could suppose that it had a serious theoretical base. But now that it has come to full expression in Bernstein's book, one cannot help exclaim with astonishment: What? Is that all you have to say? Not a shadow of an original thought! Not a single idea that was not refuted, crushed, reduced into dust by Marxism decades ago!

It was enough for opportunism to speak out in order to prove it had nothing to say. In the history of our Party that is the only importance of Bernstein's book.

Thus, saying good-bye to the mode of thought of the revolutionary proletariat, to dialectics and to the materialist conception of history, Bernstein can thank them for the attenuating circumstances they provide for his conversion. For only dialectics and the materialist conception of history, magnanimous as they are, could make Bernstein appear as an unconscious predestined instrument, by means of which the rising working class expresses its momentary weakness in order, contemptuously and with pride, to throw it aside when it sees it in the light.

---

1. *Neue Zeit*, 1897–98, vol. 18, p555.
2. Ibid., p554.

3. Van de Borght, *Handwoerterbuch der Staatsswissenschaften*, p1.

4. The mythological king of Corinth who was condemned to roll a huge stone to the top of a hill. It constantly rolled back down against making his task incessant.

5. *Vörwarts*, March 26, 1899.

6. *Vörwarts*, March 26, 1899.

7. The German revolution of 1848, which struck an effective blow against the feudal institutions in Germany.

8. see *The Communist Manifesto*, in this edition, p42.

9. see *The Communist Manifesto*, in this edition, p42.

10. see *The Communist Manifesto*, in this edition.

11. Vörwarts, March 26, 1899.

socialism and man in cuba

CHE GUEVARA

This essay was written in 1965 in the form of a letter to Carlos Quijano, editor of *Marcha*, a weekly magazine published in Montevideo, Uruguay. It was written by Che Guevara while on a three-month trip representing the revolutionary govern-ment of Cuba, during which he spoke at the United Nations and visited a number of countries in Africa.

DEAR *COMPAÑERO*:

Though belatedly, I am completing these notes in the course of my trip through Africa, hoping in this way to keep my promise. I would like to do so by dealing with the theme set forth in the title above. I think it may be of interest to Uruguayan readers.

A common argument from the mouths of capitalist spokespeople, in the ideological struggle against socialism, is that socialism, or the period of building socialism into which we have entered, is characterized by the abolition of the individual for the sake of the state. I will not try to refute this argument solely on theoretical grounds but rather to establish the facts as they exist in Cuba and then add comments of a general nature. Let me begin by broadly sketching the history of our revolutionary struggle before and after the taking of power.

As is well known, the exact date of the beginning of the revolutionary struggle — which would culminate in January 1959 — was July 26, 1953. A group led by Fidel Castro attacked the Moncada barracks in Oriente Province on the morning of that day. The attack was a failure; the failure became a disaster; and the survivors ended up in prison, beginning the revolutionary struggle again after they were freed by an amnesty.

In this process, in which there was only the germ of socialism, the individual was a fundamental factor. We put our trust in him —

individual, specific, with a first and last name — and the triumph or failure of the mission entrusted to him depended on that individual's capacity for action.

Then came the stage of guerrilla struggle. It developed in two distinct environments: the people, the still sleeping mass that had to be mobilized; and its vanguard, the guerrillas, the motor force of the mobilization, the generator of revolutionary consciousness and militant enthusiasm. This vanguard was the catalyzing agent that created the subjective conditions necessary for victory.

Here again, in the framework of the proletarianization of our thinking, of this revolution that took place in our habits and our minds, the individual was the basic factor. Every one of the combatants of the Sierra Maestra who reached an upper rank in the revolutionary forces has a record of outstanding deeds to his or her credit. They attained their rank on this basis.

This was the first heroic period, and in which combatants competed for the heaviest responsibilities, for the greatest dangers, with no other satisfaction than fulfilling a duty. In our work of revolutionary education we frequently return to this instructive theme. In the attitude of our fighters could be glimpsed the man and woman of the future.

On other occasions in our history the act of total dedication to the revolutionary cause was repeated. During the October [1962 missile] crisis and in the days of Hurricane Flora [in October 1963] we saw exceptional deeds of valor and sacrifice performed by an entire people. Finding the method to perpetuate this heroic attitude in daily life is, from the ideological standpoint, one of our fundamental tasks.

In January 1959, the Revolutionary Government was established with the participation of various members of the treacherous bourgeoisie. The presence of the Rebel Army was the basic element constituting the guarantee of power.

Serious contradictions developed right away. In the first instance, in February 1959, these were resolved when Fidel Castro assumed leadership of the government, taking the post of prime minister. This process culminated in July of the same year with the resignation under mass pressure of President Urrutia.

In the history of the Cuban Revolution there now appeared a character, well defined in its features, which would systematically reappear: the mass.

This multifaceted being is not, as is claimed, the sum of elements of the same type (reduced, moreover, to that same type by the ruling system), which acts like a flock of sheep. It is true that it follows its leaders, basically Fidel Castro, without hesitation. But the degree to which he won this trust results precisely from having interpreted the full meaning of the people's desires and aspirations, and from the sincere struggle to fulfill the promises he made.

The mass participated in the agrarian reform and in the difficult task of administering state enterprises; it went through the heroic experience of the Bay of Pigs; it was hardened in the battles against various groups of bandits armed by the CIA; it lived through one of the most important decisions of modern times during the October [missile] crisis; and today it continues to work for the building of socialism.

Viewed superficially, it might appear that those who speak of the subordination of the individual to the state are right. The mass carries out with matchless enthusiasm and discipline the tasks set by the government, whether in the field of the economy, culture, defense, sports, etc.

The initiative generally comes from Fidel, or from the revolutionary leadership, and is explained to the people, who make it their own. In some cases the party and government take a local experience and generalize it, following the same procedure.

Nevertheless, the state sometimes makes mistakes. When one of these mistakes occurs, one notes a decline in collective enthusiasm due to the effect of a quantitative diminution in each of the elements that make up the mass. Work is paralyzed until it is reduced to an insignificant level. It is time to make a correction. That is what happened in March 1962, as a result of the sectarian policy imposed on the party by Aníbal Escalante.

Clearly this mechanism is not enough to ensure a succession of sensible measures. A more structured connection with the mass is needed, and we must improve it in the course of the coming years. But as far as initiatives originating in the upper strata of the government are concerned, we are currently utilizing the almost intuitive method of sounding out general reactions to the great problems we confront.

In this Fidel is a master. His own special way of fusing himself with the people can be appreciated only by seeing him in action. At the great public mass meetings one can observe something like the dialogue of two tuning forks whose vibrations interact, producing new sounds. Fidel and the mass begin to vibrate together in a dialogue of growing intensity until they reach the climax in an abrupt conclusion crowned by our cry of struggle and victory.

The difficult thing to understand for someone not living through the experience of the revolution is this close dialectical unity between the individual and the mass, in which both are interrelated and, at the same time, in which the mass, as an aggregate of individuals, interacts with its leaders.

Some phenomena of this kind can be seen under capitalism, when politicians appear capable of mobilizing popular opinion. But when these are not genuine social movements — if they were, it would not be entirely correct to call them capitalist — they live only so long as the individual who inspires them, or until the harshness of capitalist society puts an end to the people's illusions.

In capitalist society individuals are controlled by a pitiless law usually beyond their comprehension. The alienated human specimen is tied to society as a whole by an invisible umbilical cord: the law of value. This law acts upon all aspects of one's life, shaping its course and destiny.

The laws of capitalism, which are blind and are invisible to ordinary people, act upon the individual without he or she being aware of it. One sees only the vastness of a seemingly infinite horizon ahead. That is how it is painted by capitalist propagandists who purport to draw a lesson from the example of Rockefeller — whether or not it is true — about the possibilities of individual success. The amount of poverty and suffering required for a Rockefeller to emerge, and the amount of depravity entailed in the accumulation of a fortune of such magnitude, are left out of the picture, and it is not always possible for the popular forces to expose this clearly.

(A discussion of how the workers in the imperialist countries gradually lose the spirit of working-class internationalism due to a certain degree of complicity in the exploitation of the dependent countries, and how this at the same time weakens the combativity of the masses in the imperialist countries, would be appropriate here, but that is a theme that goes beyond the scope of these notes.)

In any case, the road to success is portrayed as beset with perils — perils that, it would seem, an individual with the proper qualities can overcome to attain the goal. The reward is seen in the distance; the way is lonely. Furthermore, it is a contest among wolves. One can win only at the cost of the failure of others.

I would now like to try to define the individual, the actor in this strange and moving drama of the building of socialism, in a dual existence as a unique being and as a member of society.

I think the place to start is to recognize the individual's quality of incompleteness, of being an unfinished product. The vestiges of the past are brought into the present in one's consciousness, and a continual labor is necessary to eradicate them. The process is two-sided. On the one hand, society acts through direct and indirect education; on the other, the individual submits to a conscious process of self-education.

The new society in formation has to compete fiercely with the past. This past makes itself felt not only in one's consciousness — in which the residue of an education systematically oriented toward isolating the individual still weighs heavily — but also through the very character of this transition period in which commodity relations still persist. The commodity is the economic cell of capitalist society. So long as it exists its effects will make themselves felt in the organization of production and, consequently, in consciousness.

Marx outlined the transition period as resulting from the explosive transformation of the capitalist system destroyed by its own contradictions. In historical reality, however, we have seen that some countries that were weak limbs on the tree of imperialism were torn off first — a phenomenon foreseen by Lenin.

In these countries, capitalism had developed sufficiently to make its effects felt by the people in one way or another. But it was not capitalism's internal contradictions that, having exhausted all possibilities, caused the system to explode. The struggle for liberation from a foreign oppressor; the misery caused by external events such as war, whose consequences privileged classes place on the backs of the exploited; liberation movements aimed at overthrowing neocol-onial regimes — these are the usual factors in unleashing this kind of explosion. Conscious action does the rest.

A complete education for social labor has not yet taken place in these countries, and wealth is far from being within the reach of the masses through the simple process of appropriation. Underdevelopment, on the one hand, and the usual flight of capital, on the other, make a rapid transition without sacrifices impossible. There remains a long way to go in constructing the economic base, and the temptation is very great to follow the beaten track of material interest as the lever with which to accelerate development.

There is the danger that the forest will not be seen for the trees. The pipe dream that socialism can be achieved with the help of the dull instruments left to us by capitalism (the commodity as the economic cell, profitability, individual material interest as a lever, etc.) can lead into a blind alley. When you wind up there after having traveled a long distance with many crossroads, it is hard to figure out just where you took the wrong turn. Meanwhile, the economic foundation that has been laid has done its work of undermining the development of consciousness. To build communism it is necessary, simultaneous with the new material foundations, to build the new man and woman.

That is why it is very important to choose the right instrument for mobilizing the masses. Basically, this instrument must be moral in character, without neglecting, however, a correct use of the material incentive — especially of a social character.

As I have already said, in moments of great peril it is easy to muster a powerful response with moral incentives. Retaining their effectiveness, however, requires the development of a consciousness in which there is a new scale of values. Society as a whole must be converted into a gigantic school.

In rough outline this phenomenon is similar to the process by which capitalist consciousness was formed in its initial period. Capitalism uses force, but it also educates people in the system. Direct propaganda is carried out by those entrusted with explaining the inevitability of class society, either through some theory of divine origin or a mechanical theory of natural law. This lulls the masses, since they see themselves as being oppressed by an evil against which it is impossible to struggle.

Next comes hope of improvement — and in this, capitalism differed from the earlier caste systems, which offered no way out. For some people, the principle of the caste system will remain in effect: The reward for the obedient is to be transported after death to some fabulous other world where, according to the old beliefs, good people are rewarded. For other people there is this innovation: class divisions are determined by fate, but individuals can rise out of their class through work, initiative, etc. This process, and the myth of the self-made man, has to be profoundly hypocritical: it is the self-serving demonstration that a lie is the truth.

In our case, direct education acquires a much greater importance. The explanation is convincing because it is true; no subterfuge is needed. It is carried on by the state's educational apparatus as a function of general, technical and ideological education through such agencies as the Ministry of Education and the party's informational apparatus. Education takes hold among the masses and the foreseen new attitude tends to become a habit. The masses continue to make it their own and to influence those who have not yet educated themselves. This is the indirect form of educating the masses, as powerful as the other, structured, one.

But the process is a conscious one. Individuals continually feel the impact of the new social power and perceive that they do not entirely measure up to its standards. Under the pressure of indirect education, they try to adjust themselves to a situation that they feel is right and that their own lack of development had prevented them from reaching previously. They educate themselves.

In this period of the building of socialism we can see the new man and woman being born. The image is not yet completely finished — it never will be, since the process goes forward hand in hand with the development of new economic forms.

Aside from those whose lack of education makes them take the solitary road toward satisfying their own personal ambitions, there are those — even within this new panorama of a unified march forward — who have a tendency to walk separately from the masses accompanying them. What is important, however, is that each day individuals are acquiring ever more consciousness of the need for their incorporation into society and, at the same time, of their importance as the motor of that society.

They no longer travel completely alone over lost roads toward distant aspirations. They follow their vanguard, consisting of the party, the advanced workers, the advanced individuals who walk in unity with the masses and in close communion with them. The vanguard has its eyes fixed on the future and its reward, but this is not a vision of reward for the individual. The prize is the new society in which individuals will have different characteristics: the society of communist human beings.

The road is long and full of difficulties. At times we lose our way and must turn back. At other times we go too fast and separate ourselves from the masses. Sometimes we go too slow and feel the hot breath of those treading at our heels. In our zeal as revolutionaries we try to move ahead as fast as possible, clearing the way. But we know we must draw our nourishment from the mass and that it can advance more rapidly only if we inspire it by our example.

Despite the importance given to moral incentives, the fact that there remains a division into two main groups (excluding, of course, the minority that for one reason or another does not participate in the building of socialism) indicates the relative lack of development of social consciousness. The vanguard group is ideologically more advanced than the mass; the latter understands the new values, but not sufficiently. While among the former there has been a qualitative change that enables them to make sacrifices in their capacity as an advance guard, the latter see only part of the picture and must be subject to incentives and pressures of a certain intensity. This is the dictatorship of the proletariat operating not only on the defeated class but also on individuals of the victorious class.

All of this means that for total success a series of mechanisms, of revolutionary institutions, is needed. Along with the image of the multitudes marching toward the future comes the concept of institutionalization as a harmonious set of channels, steps, restraints and well-oiled mechanisms which facilitate the advance, which facilitate the natural selection of those destined to march in the vanguard, and which bestow rewards on those who fulfill their duties and punishments on those who commit a crime against the society that is being built.

This institutionalization of the revolution has not yet been achieved. We are looking for something new that will permit a complete identification between the government and the community in its entirety, something appropriate to the special conditions of the building of socialism, while avoiding at all costs transplanting the common-places of bourgeois democracy — such as legislative chambers, for example — into the society in formation.

Some experiments aimed at the gradual institutionalization of the revolution have been made, but without undue haste. The greatest brake has been our fear lest any appearance of formality might separate us from the masses and from the individual, which might make us lose sight of the ultimate and most important revolutionary aspiration: to see human beings liberated from their alienation.

Despite the lack of institutions, which must be overcome gradually, the masses are now making history as a conscious collective of individuals fighting for the same cause. The individual under socialism, despite apparent standardization, is more complete. Despite the lack of a perfect mechanism for it, the opportunities for self expression and making oneself felt in the social organism are infinitely greater.

It is still necessary to deepen conscious participation, individual and collective, in all the structures of management and production, and to link this to the idea of the need for technical and ideological education, so that the individual will realize that these processes are closely interdependent and their advancement is parallel. In this way the individual will reach total consciousness as a social being, which is equivalent to the full realization as a human creature, once the chains of alienation are broken.

This will be translated concretely into the reconquering of one's true nature through liberated labor, and the expression of one's own human condition through culture and art.

In order to develop a new culture, work must acquire a new status. Human beings-as-commodities cease to exist, and a system is installed that establishes a quota for the fulfillment of one's social duty. The means of production belong to society, and the machine is merely the trench where duty is performed.

A person begins to become free from thinking of the annoying fact that one needs to work to satisfy one's animal needs. Individuals start to see themselves reflected in their work and to understand their full stature as human beings through the object created, through the work accomplished. Work no longer entails surrendering a part of one's being in the form of labor power sold, which no longer belongs to the individual, but becomes an expression of oneself, a contribution to the common life in which one is reflected, the fulfillment of one's social duty.

We are doing everything possible to give work this new status as a social duty and to link it on the one hand with the development of technology, which will create the conditions for greater freedom, and on the other hand with voluntary work based on the Marxist appreciation that one truly reaches a full human condition when no longer compelled to produce by the physical necessity to sell oneself as a commodity.

Of course, there are still coercive aspects to work, even when it is voluntary. We have not transformed all the coercion that surrounds us into conditioned reflexes of a social character and, in many cases, is still produced under the pressures of one's environment. (Fidel calls this moral compulsion.) There is still a need to undergo a complete spiritual rebirth in one's attitude toward one's own work, freed from the direct pressure of the social environment, though linked to it by new habits. That will be communism.

The change in consciousness does not take place automatically, just as change in the economy does not take place automatically. The alterations are slow and not rhythmic; there are periods of acceleration, periods that are slower, and even retrogressions.

Furthermore, we must take into account, as I pointed out before, that we are not dealing with a period of pure transition, as Marx envisaged in his *Critique of the Gotha Program*, but rather with a new phase unforeseen by him: an initial period of the transition to communism, or of the construction of socialism. This transition is taking place in the midst of violent class struggles, and with elements of capitalism within it that obscure a complete understanding of its essence.

If we add to this the scholasticism that has held back the development of Marxist philosophy and impeded a systematic treatment of the transition period, whose political economy has not yet been developed, we must agree that we are still in diapers and that it is necessary to devote ourselves to investigating all the principal characteristics of this period before elaborating an economic and political theory of greater scope.

The resulting theory will, no doubt, put great stress on the two pillars of the construction of socialism: the education of the new man and woman and the development of technology. Much remains to be done in regard to both, but delay is least excusable in regard to the concept of technology as a basic foundation, since this is not a question of going forward blindly but of following a long stretch of road already opened up by the world's more advanced countries. This is why Fidel pounds away with such insistence on the need for the technological and scientific training of our people and especially of its vanguard.

In the field of ideas that do not lead to activities involving production, it is easier to see the division between material and spiritual necessity. For a long time individuals have been trying to free themselves from alienation through culture and art. While a person dies every day during the eight or more hours in which he or she functions as a commodity, individuals come to life afterward in their spiritual creations. But this remedy bears the germs of the same sickness: that of a solitary being seeking harmony with the world. One defends one's individuality, which is oppressed by the environment, and reacts to aesthetic ideas as a unique being whose aspiration is to remain immaculate. It is nothing more than an attempt to escape. The law of value is no longer simply a reflection of the relations of production; the monopoly capitalists — even while employing purely empirical methods — surround that law with a complicated scaffolding that turns it into a docile servant. The superstructure imposes a kind of art in which the artist must be educated. Rebels are subdued by the machine, and only exceptional talents may create their own work. The rest become shamefaced hirelings or are crushed.

A school of artistic experimentation is invented, which is said to be the definition of freedom; but this "experimentation" has its limits, imperceptible until there is a clash, that is, until the real problems of individual alienation arise. Meaningless anguish or vulgar amusement thus become convenient safety valves for human anxiety. The idea of using art as a weapon of protest is combated.

Those who play by the rules of the game are showered with honors — such honors as a monkey might get for performing pirouettes. The condition is that one does not try to escape from the invisible cage.

When the revolution took power there was an exodus of those who had been completely housebroken. The rest — whether they were revolutionaries or not — saw a new road. Artistic inquiry experienced a new impulse. The paths, however, had already been more or less laid out, and the escapist concept hid itself behind the word "freedom." This attitude was often found even among the revolutionaries themselves, a reflection in their consciousness of bourgeois idealism.

In countries that have gone through a similar process, attempts have been made to combat such tendencies with an exaggerated dogmatism. General culture became virtually taboo, and the acme of cultural aspiration was declared to be the formally exact representation of nature. This was later transformed into a mechanical representation of the social reality they wanted to show: the ideal society, almost without conflicts or contradictions, that they sought to create.

Socialism is young and has its mistakes. We revolutionaries often lack the knowledge and intellectual audacity needed to meet the task of developing the new man and woman with methods different from the conventional ones; conventional methods suffer from the influences of the society that created them. (Once again the theme of the relationship between form and content is posed.) Disorientation is widespread, and the problems of material construction absorb us. There are no artists of great authority who also have great revolutionary authority. The members of the party must take this task in hand and seek the achievement of the main goal: to educate the people.

What is sought then is simplification, something everyone can understand, something functionaries understand. True artistic experimentation ends, and the problem of general culture is reduced to assimilating the socialist present and the dead (therefore, not dangerous) past. Thus socialist realism arises upon the foundations of the art of the last century.

The realistic art of the 19th century, however, also has a class character, more purely capitalist perhaps than the decadent art of the 20th century that reveals the anguish of the alienated individual. In the field of culture, capitalism has given all that it had to give, and nothing remains but the stench of a corpse, today's decadence in art.

But why try to find the only valid prescription in the frozen forms of socialist realism? We cannot counterpose "freedom" to socialist realism, because the former does not yet exist and will not exist until the complete development of the new society. We must not, from the pontifical throne of realism-at-all-costs, condemn all art forms since the first half of the 19th century, for we would then fall into the Proudhonian mistake of going back to the past, of putting a strait-jacket on the artistic expression of the people who are being born and are in the process of making themselves.

What is needed is the development of an ideological-cultural mechanism that permits both free inquiry and the uprooting of the weeds that multiply so easily in the fertilized soil of state subsidies.

In our country the error of mechanical realism has not appeared, but rather its opposite. This is because the need for the creation of a new individual has not been understood, a new human being who would represent neither the ideas of the 19th century nor those of our own decadent and morbid century.

What we must create is the human being of the 21st century, although this is still a subjective aspiration, not yet systematized. This is precisely one of the fundamental objectives of our study and our work. To the extent that we achieve concrete success on a theoretical plane — or, vice versa, to the extent that we draw theoretical conclusions of a broad character on the basis of our concrete research — we will have made a valuable contribution to Marxism-Leninism, to the cause of humanity.

By reacting against the human being of the 19th century we have relapsed into the decadence of the 20th century. It is not a very grave error, but we must overcome it lest we leave open the door for revisionism.

The great multitudes continue to develop. The new ideas are gaining a good momentum within society. The material possibilities for the integrated development of absolutely all members of society make the task much more fruitful. The present is a time of struggle; the future is ours.

To sum up, the fault of many of our artists and intellectuals lies in their original sin: they are not true revolutionaries. We can try to graft the elm tree so that it will bear pears, but at the same time we must plant pear trees. New generations will come that will be free of original sin. The probability that great artists will appear will be greater to the degree that the field of culture and the possibilities for expression are broadened.

Our task is to prevent the current generation, torn asunder by its conflicts, from becoming perverted and from perverting new generations. We must not create either docile servants of official thought, or "scholarship students" who live at the expense of the state — practicing freedom in quotation marks. Revolutionaries will come who will sing the song of the new man and woman in the true voice of the people. This is a process that takes time.

In our society the youth and the party play a big part. The former is especially important because it is the malleable clay from which the new person can be built with none of the old defects. The youth are treated in accordance with our aspirations. Their education is every day more complete, and we do not neglect their incorporation into work from the outset. Our scholarship students do physical work during their vacations or along with their studies. Work is a reward in some cases, a means of education in others, but it is never a punishment. A new generation is being born.

The party is a vanguard organization. It is made up of the best workers, who are proposed for membership by their fellow workers. It is a minority, but it has great authority because of the quality of its cadres. Our aspiration is for the party to become a mass party, but only when the masses have reached the level of the vanguard, that is, when they are educated for communism.

Our work constantly strives toward this education. The party is the living example; its cadres must teach hard work and sacrifice. By their action, they must lead the masses to the completion of the revolutionary task, which involves years of hard struggle against the difficulties of construction, class enemies, the maladies of the past, imperialism.

Now, I would like to explain the role played by the personality, by men and women as individuals leading the masses that make history. This is our experience; it is not a prescription.

Fidel gave the revolution its impulse in the first years, and also its leadership. He always set its tone; but there is a good group of revolutionaries who are developing along the same road as the central leader. And there is a great mass that follows its leaders because it has faith in them. It has faith in those leaders because they have known how to interpret its aspirations.

It is not a matter of how many kilograms of meat one has to eat, or of how many times a year someone can go to the beach, or how many pretty things from abroad you might be able to buy with present-day wages. It is a matter of making the individual feel more complete, with much more inner wealth and much more responsibility.

People in our country know that the glorious period in which they happen to live is one of sacrifice; they are familiar with sacrifice. The first ones came to know it in the Sierra Maestra and wherever they fought; later, everyone in Cuba came to know it. Cuba is the vanguard of America and must make sacrifices because it occupies the post of advance guard, because it shows the masses of Latin America the road to full freedom.

Within the country the leadership has to carry out its vanguard role. It must be said with all sincerity that in a real revolution, to which one gives his or her all and from which one expects no material reward, the task of the vanguard revolutionary is both magnificent and agonizing.

At the risk of seeming ridiculous, let me say that the true revolutionary is guided by great feelings of love. It is impossible to think of a genuine revolutionary lacking this quality. Perhaps it is one of the great dramas of the leader that he or she must combine a passionate spirit with a cold intelligence and make painful decisions without flinching. Our vanguard revolutionaries must idealize this love of the people, of the most sacred causes, and make it one and indivisible. They cannot descend, with small doses of daily affection, to the level where ordinary people put their love into practice.

The leaders of the revolution have children just beginning to talk, who are not learning to say "daddy"; their wives, too, must be part of the general sacrifice of their lives in order to take the revolution to its destiny. The circle of their friends is limited strictly to the circle of comrades in the revolution. There is no life outside of it.

In these circumstances one must have a large dose of humanity, a large dose of a sense of justice and truth in order to avoid dogmatic extremes, cold scholasticism, or an isolation from the masses. We must strive every day so that this love of living humanity is transformed into actual deeds, into acts that serve as examples, as a moving force.

The revolutionary, the ideological motor force of the revolution within the party, is consumed by this uninterrupted activity that comes to an end only with death, unless the construction of socialism is accomplished on a world scale. If one's revolutionary zeal is blunted when the most urgent tasks have been accomplished on a local scale and one forgets about proletarian internationalism, the revolution one leads will cease to be a driving force and sink into a comfortable drowsiness that imperialism, our irreconcilable enemy, will utilize to gain ground. Proletarian internationalism is a duty, but it is also a revolutionary necessity. This is the way we educate our people.

Of course there are dangers in the present situation, and not only that of dogmatism, not only that of freezing the ties with the masses midway in the great task. There is also the danger of the weaknesses we can fall into. The way is open to infection by the germs of future corruption if a person thinks that dedicating his or her entire life to the revolution means that, in return, one should not be distracted by such worries as that one's child lacks certain things, that one's children's shoes are worn out, that one's family lacks some necessity.

In our case we have maintained that our children must have, or lack, those things that the children of the ordinary citizen have or lack; our families should understand this and struggle for it to be that way. The revolution is made through human beings, but individuals must forge their revolutionary spirit day by day.

Thus we march on. At the head of the immense column — we are neither ashamed nor afraid to say it — is Fidel. After him come the best cadres of the party, and immediately behind them, so close that we feel its tremendous force, comes the people in its entirety, a solid structure of individual beings moving toward a common goal, men and women who have attained consciousness of what must be done, people who fight to escape from the realm of necessity and to enter that of freedom.

This great throng organizes itself; its organization results from its consciousness of the necessity of this organization. It is no longer a dispersed force, divisible into thousands of fragments thrown into the air like splinters from a hand grenade, trying by any means to achieve some protection from an uncertain future, in desperate struggle with their fellows.

We know that sacrifices lie ahead and that we must pay a price for the heroic fact that we are, as a nation, a vanguard. We, as leaders, know that we must pay a price for the right to say that we are at the head of a people that is at the head of America. Each and every one of us readily pays his or her quota of sacrifice, conscious of being rewarded with the satisfaction of fulfilling a duty, conscious of advancing with everyone toward the new man and woman glimpsed on the horizon.

Allow me to draw some conclusions:

We socialists are freer because we are more fulfilled; we are more fulfilled because we are freer.

The skeleton of our complete freedom is already formed. The flesh and the clothing are lacking; we will create them.

Our freedom and its daily sustenance are paid for in blood and sacrifice.

Our sacrifice is a conscious one: an installment paid on the freedom that we are building.

The road is long and, in part, unknown. We recognize our limitations. We will make the human being of the 21st century — we, ourselves.

We will forge ourselves in daily action, creating a new man and woman with a new technology.

Individuals play a role in mobilizing and leading the masses insofar as they embody the highest virtues and aspirations of the people and do not wander from the path.

Clearing the way is the vanguard group, the best among the good, the party.

The basic clay of our work is the youth; we place our hope in it and prepare it to take the banner from our hands.

If this inarticulate letter clarifies anything, it has accomplished the objective that motivated it. Accept our ritual greeting — which is like a handshake or an "Ave Maria Puríssima":

Patria o muerte! [Homeland or death!]

karl marx & friedrich engels

Karl Marx (1818–83) was born to a German family in Trier. While studying law and philosophy in Bonn and Berlin he was influenced by Hegel, but was soon drawn to the study of political economy. After an active role in the revolutions of 1848, he fled into exile first to Paris and then London where he lived for the rest of his life. In 1864 he co-founded the International Workingmen's Association which, among other activities, organized solidarity with the Paris Commune in 1871, the independence movement in Poland and campaigned for an end to slavery. His major work on political economy, *Capital*, was first published in 1867.

Friedrich Engels (1820–95) was raised a devout Calvinist in the Rhineland. He moved to Britain in 1842 to run his father's textile business in Manchester where he witnessed the social impact of the industrial revolution. In 1848 Engels joined Marx on the *Neue Rheinische Zeitung* which became an important voice of the revolutionary movement that shook Europe during that year. Exiled to Britain in 1850, Engels continued his political collaboration with Marx, and together they wrote numerous books on social theory, political economy, philosophy and history. Engels edited the second and third volumes of *Capital* after Marx's death, and his own work on dialectical materialism and on the oppression of women in class society remain significant contributions to revolutionary theory.

rosa luxemburg

Born in Warsaw in 1871, Rosa Luxemburg became a prominent leader of the European socialist movement. A political activist while still in high school, she attended university in Zurich where women were admitted on an equal basis with men. Living in Switzerland she first encountered Marxism and some of the leading Russian revolutionary exiles.

Outspoken in her opposition to militarism and the German Social Democratic Party's capitulation to nationalism in World War I, Luxemburg was imprisoned for her beliefs on several occasions. She welcomed the Russian Revolution of 1917, and in an extensive dialogue with Lenin, she argued for revolutionary democratic socialism and a humanist approach to Marxism. She wrote extensively on history, philosophy, political economy and labor struggles, and was known for her brilliant oratory at party meetings and mass rallies.

She was assassinated along with Karl Liebknecht in January 1919 by proto-fascist forces in the immediate aftermath of a popular uprising in Berlin.

A Polish Jew and a brave and brilliant woman Rosa Luxemburg challenged every convention of her time. She remains one of the most important Marxist thinkers of the 20th century, and her internationalism, her sharp critique of militarism and the global rise of capitalism offer invaluable insights to today's world.

che guevara

One of *Time* magazine's "icons of the century," Ernesto Guevara de la Serna was born in Argentina on June 14, 1928. He made several trips around Latin America during and immediately after his studies at medical school in Buenos Aires, including his 1952 journey written up in the famous notes known as *The Motorcycle Diaries*.

While he was living in Guatemala, in 1954, the elected government of Jacobo Arbenz was overthrown in a CIA-organized coup. Ernesto escaped to Mexico, profoundly radicalized. In July 1955 Guevara met Fidel Castro and immediately enlisted in the guerrilla expedition to overthrow Cuban dictator Fulgencio Batista. The Cubans nicknamed him "Che." After the Cuban Revolution of January 1, 1959, Guevara became a key leader of the new revolutionary government, representing Cuba around the world and at international forums.

As had been his intention since joining the Cuban revolutionary movement, Guevara left Cuba in April 1965, initially to lead a guerrilla mission to support the revolutionary struggle in the Congo. He returned to Cuba secretly in December 1965, to prepare another guerrilla force for Bolivia that would extend the revolutionary movement in Latin America. He was wounded and captured by U.S.-trained and run Bolivian counterinsurgency troops on October 8, 1967. The following day he was murdered and his body hidden.

adrienne rich

Adrienne Rich was born in Baltimore in the United States in 1929. Since the selection in 1951 of her first volume by W.H. Auden for the Yale Younger Poets Prize, her work has evolved from closed forms to a poetics of change, rooted in a radical imagination and politics. Her books of poetry include *Collected Early Poems 1950-1970*; *The Fact of a Doorframe: Selected Poems 1950-2001*; *The Dream of a Common Language*; *Your Native Land, Your Life*; *An Atlas of the Difficult World*; *Dark Fields of the Republic*; *Midnight Salvage*; and *Fox*. Prose works include *Of Woman Born: Motherhood as Experience and Institution*; *On Lies, Secrets and Silence*; *Blood, Bread and Poetry*; *What Is Found There: Notebooks on Poetry and Politics* (1993, new edition 2003) and *Arts of the Possible: Essays and Conversations*. Her latest volume of poetry is *The School Among the Ruins: Poems 2000-2004*.

Her work has received many awards including the Ruth Lilly Prize, the Wallace Stevens Award, the Los Angeles Times Book Award, the Lambda Literary Award, the Lenore Marshall/Nation Award, a MacArthur Fellowship, the Lannan Literary Foundation Lifetime Achievement Award and the Bollingen Prize.

armando hart

A founding member of the July 26 Movement in Cuba, Armando Hart (born in 1930) was an underground activist in the struggle against the Batista dictatorship. He was arrested and jailed, and only released following a prisoners' rebellion in the days after the January 1959 Cuban Revolution. He was named as minister of education in the revolutionary government and led the nationwide literacy campaign. Later (1976-97) he became minister of culture. His partner, Haydée Santamaría, was founder of the well-respected Latin American cultural institution, Casa de las Américas. Hart is the author of numerous essays, articles and books on culture and cultural policy, history and social development. These include: *La cultura en el proceso de integración de América Latina; Del trabajo cultural; Cambiar las reglas del juego; Cultura en revolución; Hacia una dimensión cultural del desarrollo; Mi visión del Che desde los '90s;* and *Perfiles.* He has received many awards for his writings and work, both in Cuba and Latin America. Hart was the director of the José Martí Institute, Havana, a deputy to Cuba's National Assembly and a member of the Council of State, before passing in 2017.

CHE GUEVARA BOOKS PUBLISHED BY
SEVEN STORIES PRESS

The Motorcycle Diaries: Notes on a Latin American Journey

Introductions by Walter Salles and Cintio Vitier
Foreword by Aleida Guevara

"The enormity of our endeavor escaped us in those moments; all we could see was the dust on the road ahead and ourselves on the bike, devouring kilometers in our flight northward," wrote a young Ernesto Guevara as he and his buddy Alberto Granado hit the road on a vintage Norton motorcycle to discover Latin America.

This is his lively and highly entertaining diary of that adventure, featuring exclusive, unpublished photos taken by the 23-year-old Argentine medical student on his journey across a continent, and a tender foreword by Aleida Guevara offering an insightful perspective on her father—the man and the icon. (July 2021). ISBN: 978-1-64421-068-0

The Bolivian Diary

Introduction by Fidel Castro
Foreword by Camilo Guevara

Che's account of the fateful Bolivia mission that attempted to spark a continent-wide revolution. This is Che Guevara's last diary, compiled from the notebooks discovered when he was captured and executed by the Bolivian army in October 1967. It became an instant bestseller. This newly revised edition has an insightful preface by Che's eldest son Camilo, a chronology, maps, and 32 pages of rare or unpublished photos. (December 2021). ISBN: 978-1-64421-074-1

Congo Diary: Episodes of the Revolutionary War in the Congo

Foreword by Aleida Guevara
Introductions by Gabriel García Márquez and Roberto Saviano

Che Guevara's intriguing account of the revolutionary war in the Congo, filling in the missing chapter in his life. Prior to his fateful mission to Bolivia, in 1965 Che led a secret Cuban force that went to aid the African national liberation movement against the Belgian colonialists, after the assassination of Patrice Lumumba by the CIA. (November 2021). ISBN: 978-1-64421-072-7

I Embrace You with All My Revolutionary Fervor: Letters 1947–1967

Foreword by Aleida Guevara

Ernesto Che Guevara was a voyager—and thus a letter writer—for his entire adult life. The letters collected here range from letters home during his *Motorcycle Diaries* trip, to the long letter to Fidel after the success of the Cuban revolution in early 1959, from the most personal to the intensely political, revealing someone who not only thought deeply about everything he encountered, but for whom the process of social transformation was a constant companion from his youth until shortly before his death. His letters give us Che the son, the friend, the lover, the guerrilla fighter, the political leader, the philosopher, the poet. Che in these letters is often playful, funny, sometimes sarcastic, and deeply affectionate. His life was short, and these twenty years, from when he was nineteen until days before his death, show it was also incredibly rich and full. (November 2021). ISBN: 978-1-64421-095-6

Latin America Diaries:
The Sequel to *The Motorcycle Diaries*

This sequel to *The Motorcycle Diaries* includes letters, poetry, and journalism that document young Ernesto Guevara's second Latin American journey following his graduation from medical school in 1953. It reveals how the young Argentine is transformed into a militant revolutionary, ready to commit himself to the guerrilla struggle Fidel Castro and his compañeros are about to launch in Cuba against the dictatorship of General Fulgencio Batista. (September 2024). ISBN: 978-1-64421-100-7

Reminiscences of the Cuban Revolutionary War

Foreword by Aleida Guevara

Originally published a series of articles for Cuban papers, this thoroughly revised edition includes for the first time corrections made by Che himself to his diary on which he based the essays. This book also includes a foreword by Che's daughter Aleidita about how her parents met during the revolutionary war and 32 pages of photos and maps of the guerrilla campaign. (March 2025). ISBN: 978-1-64421-107-6

Che Guevara Reader:
Writings on Politics & Revolution

Edited by David Deutschmann and María del Carmen Ariet García

Recognized as one of *Time*'s "icons of the 20th century," Che Guevara became a legend in his own time and has now reemerged as a symbol of a new generation of political activists. Far more than a guerrilla strategist, Che Guevara made a profound and lasting contribution to revolutionary theory and Marxist humanism as demonstrated in this bestselling book. (June 2022). ISBN: 978-1-64421-112-0

Global Justice: Three Essays on Liberation and Socialism
Introduction by María del Carmen Ariet García

Is there an alternative to the corporate globalization and militarism that is ravaging our planet? These classic works by Ernesto Che Guevara present a revolutionary view of a different world in which human solidarity and understanding replace imperialist aggression and exploitation. (June 2024). ISBN: 978-1-64421-156-4

Guerrilla Warfare: Authoritative, Revised New Edition
Foreword by Harry "Pombo" Villegas

A bestselling classic for decades, this is Che Guevara's own incisive analysis of the Cuban revolution—a text studied by his admirers and adversaries alike. Although often regarded as a "manual" for guerrilla warfare, this book is primarily a political account of what happened in Cuba and why, explaining how a small group of dedicated fighters grew in strength with the support of the Cuban people, overcoming their limitations to defeat the US-backed dictator's army. He also analyzes why the Cuban revolution attained a "continental and international transcendence." (November 2024). ISBN: 978-1-64421-146-5

The Awakening of Latin America
Edited by María del Carmen Ariet García

In a letter to his mother in 1954, a young Ernesto Guevara wrote, "The Americas will be the theater of my adventures in a way that is much more significant than I would have believed." In *The Awakening of Latin America* we have the story of those adventures, charting Che's evolution from an impressionable young medical student to the "heroic guerrilla," assassinated in cold blood in Bolivia. Spanning seventeen years, this anthology draws on from his family's personal archives and offers the best of Che's writing: examples of his journalism, essays, speeches, letters, and even poems. As Che documents his early travels through Latin America, his involvement in the Guatemalan and Cuban revolutions, and his rise to international prominence under Fidel Castro, we see how his fervent commitment to social justice shaped and was shaped by the continent he called home.

Nearly half of this book is published for the first time and pre-dates Che's arrival in Cuba with Fidel Castro's guerrilla expedition in 1956. Also included are his notes for his unfinished book, *The Social Role of Doctors in Latin America*. (July 2024). ISBN: 978-1-64421-164-9